BEYOND STANDARDS

BEYOND STANDARDS

THE FRAGMENTATION OF EDUCATION GOVERNANCE AND THE PROMISE OF CURRICULUM REFORM

MORGAN POLIKOFF

HARVARD EDUCATION PRESS
CAMBRIDGE, MASSACHUSETTS

Paperback ISBN 978-1-68253-611-7
Library Edition ISBN 978-1-68253-612-4

Library of Congress Cataloging-in-Publication Data is on file.

Published by Harvard Education Press,
an imprint of the Harvard Education Publishing Group
Harvard Education Press
8 Story Street
Cambridge, MA 02138

Cover Design: Wilcox Design
Cover Image: filo/DigitalVision Vectors via Getty Images.

The typefaces in this book are Minion Pro, Stone Sans, and Alte DIN 1451.

CONTENTS

CHAPTER 1

The Best-Laid Plans

For thirty years, standards have been at the heart of education reform efforts. Every seven to ten years over that period, committees of experts have gotten together to write new standards for states to adopt. Districts have selected new curriculum materials and offered teachers professional development. Teachers have worked with colleagues to understand the standards and go about the hard work of doing their best to implement them in the classroom. Kids have taken tests to gauge their progress. Scores have risen and fallen. Gaps have narrowed and widened. Every other year samples of kids have taken the National Assessment of Educational Progress and pundits have read the trends to conclude that, yes, things are getting better (or, of late, no, not so much).

Why do we do all this work? The argument for the standards movement is pretty straightforward and is best laid out in a now-seminal piece by Marshall S. Smith and Jennifer O'Day called "Systemic School Reform."[1] Smith and O'Day summarize the school reforms of the 1980s and argue that they've mostly failed to achieve their goals of improving schools at scale. They lay out the case for a systemic education policy reform agenda focused on standards. It is the clearest intellectual argument to justify the last thirty years of standards-based reform in American education.

The remarkable thing about "Systemic School Reform" and the argument it advances is that almost the entire first half of it—the part where the authors catalog the flaws of existing reform agendas and diagnose the structural issues in American education—could be written today with essentially no edits. Smith and O'Day were right about the problems of American education, and their diagnosis of the problems is stunningly accurate and relevant to our current problems thirty years later.

The questions this book sets out to address are straightforward ones. Have standards failed? If they have, why? What can we do to right the boat? Or is it a lost cause and we should cut bait?

What this book argues is that the proponents of standards-based reform—starting with its academic advocates but carrying through to its champions in governors' mansions, statehouses, and even teacher union headquarters—gave away the farm when they moved from correctly diagnosing our educational woes to designing and implementing a policy to solve those problems. What we've ended up with—the standards movement as we know it and have experienced it—is completely inadequate to the goal of bringing about educational equity or excellence. Standards-based reform policies have hardly challenged the very structures that cause educational failure. These policies use almost magical thinking about how educational systems in fifty states and thirteen thousand districts would respond to a reform as weak as standards-plus-tests-and-modest-accountability. The results of this work have been disappointing, and there is no reason to believe that tinkering with policy design will meaningfully change the outcomes.

So what do we do now? If standards aren't working and will not work, how can we improve teaching and learning at scale? The book makes a two-part argument. First, it argues that only a reform that gets much closer to the classroom—curriculum materials—has a hope of meaningfully moving the needle on instruction. Standards are just too far from actual teaching for us to hope that educators can consistently interpret and implement them in ways that align with the standards' intent. Second, it argues that even a curriculum-oriented instructional reform will not get us where we need to be if we do not also challenge educational structures that impede reform, segregate students, and deprive our most disadvantaged students of the resources and teachers they need to succeed. These structures primarily include radically decentralized school districts, undemocratic school boards, and teacher policies that often incentivize the best teachers to teach in the most advantaged areas. In other words, bringing instructional reform down to the classroom through curriculum materials can result in more instructional progress than we have seen, but even that will not be enough to get us where we need to go.

WHAT WAS WRONG WITH AMERICAN EDUCATION THAT STANDARDS WERE SUPPOSED TO FIX?

The Goal—Good Schools for All Children

With at most modest exceptions, the goals laid out in "Systemic School Reform" that animated the standards movement were goals that everyone would still support today. We all want a system that offers effective schools to all children, and hardly anyone could disagree with indicators like the following:

- A fairly stable staff, made up of enthusiastic and caring teachers who have a mastery both of the subject matter of the curriculum and of a variety of pedagogies for teaching it
- A well thought through, challenging curriculum that is integrated across grade levels and is appropriate for the range of experiences, cultures, and abilities of the students
- A high level of teacher and student engagement in the educational mission of the school—not just for the high achievers but for the vast majority of students
- Opportunities for parents to support and participate in the education of their children
- A schoolwide vision or mission and common instructional goals that tie the content, structure, and resources of the school together into an effective, unified whole
- A school climate that is conducive to teaching and learning, that both contains the resources and embodies the common purpose and mutual respect necessary for them to be successful

There are perhaps modest ways in which these goals might be tweaked if they were written today. For instance, cultural relevance and attention to educational equity would likely be foregrounded more directly, as would nonacademic or social-emotional goals. But in all, almost everyone would have agreed then and would still agree today that if all students had access to schools with these attributes we would be much better off.

OUTCOME PROBLEMS

The reality in the 1980s was seen as quite far from this lofty goal of a quality school for all children. When the standards movement was burgeoning, advocates were driven first and foremost by concerns about student achievement. The famous 1983 report *A Nation at Risk* laid out these concerns bluntly.[2] The report argued that achievement was low when compared with other countries, and that it had declined since the Sputnik-fueled craze of the 1950s. The report cited large numbers of adults and modest numbers of high school graduates with functional illiteracy, unable to perform even the basic functions of entry-level positions in business and industry. The report concluded in now famously stark terms: "If an unfriendly foreign power had attempted to impose on America the mediocre educational performance that exists today, we might well have viewed it as an act of war. As it stands, we have allowed this to happen to ourselves."[3]

A Nation at Risk did not focus as strongly on gaps in performance or opportunity (indeed, the word "gap" doesn't appear in the document), but these gaps emerged as a focus over the ensuing decade, and they featured prominently in 1990s-era thinking about the rationale for standards-based reforms.[4] As standards-based reforms became folded into federal law through Title I (itself a program aimed at eradicating opportunity gaps for low-income students), the gap-orientation of the policy became more prominent.

THE REASONS FOR POOR PERFORMANCE

So why didn't we have a quality school for every child, and why, therefore, was achievement not what we wanted it to be?[5] First and foremost, advocates for standards focused their attention on educational systems and structures, which they decried as fragmented and overly complex. One hundred thousand schools, thirteen thousand districts and school boards, fifty states with both legislative and executive authorities involved, and a federal Department of Education on top of it (not to mention the courts) are hardly a recipe for coherence and consistency. And these are merely the organizations and structures that have formal authority—there are also informal sources of authority and guidance from teacher education programs to curriculum creators and providers to unions to parent organizations to teachers' own professional networks. Altogether, these structures send teachers myriad—and often conflicting—messages about what they should be doing in the classroom.

Second, advocates argued that the purposes of schooling were not always clear or agreed upon. At the macro level, there are debates about whether the purpose of education is primarily academic, or whether the purpose also extends to social, emotional, civic, or other desired outcomes. At a more micro level, there is of course disagreement about what particular content and skills to emphasize (see, for instance, the well-publicized and never-ending reading and math wars).[6] There is also more fundamental disagreement about the proper locus of control for decisions about what to teach students—whether it lies with teachers or at a higher level.[7]

Third, advocates argued that the political pressures and realities of education politics get in the way of sustained vision and long-term thinking. For example, school boards are typically elected on short cycles of just a few years (ditto for governors, mayors, and legislators). If they are trying to demonstrate that they have accomplished something worthy of reelection, they will be likely to favor short-term gains and low-hanging fruit over sustained and more difficult forms of reform. This contributes to a quick-fix, silver-bullet mentality, rather than an approach that recognizes the necessity for slow, long-term thinking.

Together, the advocates argued, these weaknesses led to the challenges they observed in the schools of the time. Curriculum materials were weak and diffuse, because publishers couldn't create a more focused and coherent approach if it would apply in only one state or a small handful of districts. Professional development and learning (both preservice and in-service) were limited and focused on general skills because they could not be more focused without clear and common goals. Assessments were poorly aligned with what teachers were actually teaching because it was impossible for them to be otherwise—there was no common instructional core to guide assessment and evaluation of student progress. And teacher supports (e.g., time and space to collaborate and reflect) were weak and variable, with the worst supports in the most disadvantaged settings. As a result of all these limitations, American teachers were conservative in their instructional practice—falling back on the content and practices they experienced in their own education and rarely attempting more ambitious instructional reform.

HOW STANDARDS WOULD FIX AMERICAN EDUCATION

How could we fix these large, structural problems and improve American education at scale?[8] The solution proposed by standards advocates and policy reformers was to exercise the authority of the state, rightly recognizing that reform at scale could happen only through higher-level leadership, and lead with a clear set of goals and visions. At the center of these goals, they argued, must be clear expectations for what students should be learning in school—what we call content standards (the standards in standards-based reform). In short, the theory of change underlying standards-based reform went something like this.

First, states should assemble experts to come together and agree what students should know and be able to do at the end of their educational experience. They should work backward from this end goal to spell out the progression of student knowledge across grades. In early versions of this policy theory, advocates recommended standards be spelled out in four-year chunks, and in the pre–No Child Left Behind (NCLB) era content standards were indeed often constructed in grade spans rather than grade by grade.[9]

Second, states should work to support schools and districts to adopt or create high-quality curriculum materials aligned with the standards. One way to increase the odds of this happening would be for states to hold statewide adoptions where they verified the quality of an approved list of aligned materials. But the advocates argued that states must ultimately leave curriculum adoption decisions (including the decision to purchase a material not approved by the state, or to create materials from scratch) in the hands of local actors.

Third, states would reform preservice and in-service teacher professional learning opportunities. Noting that preservice teacher education was mostly provided by fiercely independent colleges of education, these early advocates envisioned that states might regulate teacher knowledge of standards through performance assessment of teacher knowledge or competency at the end of their training period. For in-service training, these advocates simply noted that states could either directly create training opportunities aligned with standards or offer contracts or incentives for subunits to do so. Either way, they argued, the amount and quality of preservice professional learning would need to be dramatically increased.

Fourth, states would need to reorient their assessment systems toward the content in the standards and away from more general basic skills assessment. Coupled with modest external accountability policies, standards-aligned assessment would serve two purposes. It would give educators and the general public a clear understanding of student progress toward mastering the content in the standards. And it would send clear messages to teachers about what they should be teaching and offer some external incentive for them to want to teach it. Again, in early versions of standards-based reform, assessment was done in grade spans. In the NCLB era and since, students have been tested more frequently.[10]

Fifth and final, depending on the particular instantiation of standards-based reform we are talking about, its advocates envisioned some degree of restructuring of authority among the different levels in the education system. For instance, Smith and O'Day talked about the key roles at the school, district, and state levels in their argument for systemic standards-based reform.

The theory by which this policy will result in better outcomes for children, then, is relatively straightforward. A stylized version is presented in figure 1.1. Standards come first—they set the goal and vision (perhaps not just content standards, but also other standards or expectations for the kinds of outcomes schools should achieve). These are reinforced through curriculum materials, professional learning, and assessments, each of which are aligned with standards. Governance structures are cleared out or simplified as needed to minimize conflicting messages. Teachers implement the standards in the classroom. Students learn the standards and achieve the other goals set out by the system.

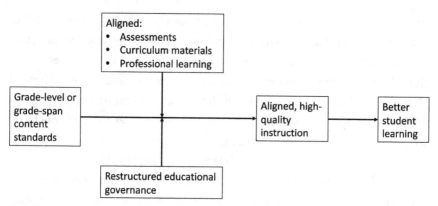

FIGURE 1.1.   A stylized theory of change for standards-based reforms.

It sounds simple and straightforward. But it hasn't worked. In the rest of this chapter I offer some thoughts on what's right and what's wrong with this theory of change and lay out the path for the rest of the book.

WHAT'S RIGHT IN THE STANDARDS-BASED REFORM THEORY OF CHANGE

There are many core elements of this argument that were correct at the time they were first being made. And, to a large extent, what was true when these reforms were first put forth remains true today. For starters, student outcomes were not what they should have been. The language of *A Nation at Risk* was surely overwrought, but the principle—that academic performance in US schools was mediocre at best—was certainly true then.[11] Just as a few data points:

- In the mid-1980s, only about 74 percent of US adults had high school degrees or higher, and about 21 percent had college degrees or higher.
- In the first wave of the National Assessment of Educational Progress in 1992, just 29 percent of students scored proficient at fourth- and eighth-grade reading, and 18–21 percent of students scored proficient at fourth- and eighth-grade mathematics.
- On the Second International Mathematics Study, US students scored at or below the international average both in eighth grade and at age 17 on a range of mathematical topics, far behind high-achieving countries like Japan.

While one can quibble with the individual indicators used in *A Nation at Risk*, it is hard to argue with the overall conclusion that educational outcomes at that time were not where they needed to be.

For another thing, instruction in US schools could be improved, and poor-quality instruction almost certainly contributes to the low levels of performance and larger-than-desired gaps that we observe. This was certainly true in the 1980s and 1990s when these policies were first being pushed, and it remains true today. There are a number of dimensions along which instruction fell short around that time. For example, large proportions of students did not have access to the kinds of courses they needed to prepare them for college. Instruction was criticized as "[containing] little depth or coherence, emphasizing facts and basic skills over opportunities to analyze and solve problems."[12] And heavily tracked schools resulted in sharply unequal educational opportunities.[13]

The diagnoses—the contributing factors to poor instruction—were also largely correct. Educational governance was indeed outrageously complex. In describing the governance structure for California as of 2007 (so quite a bit after the onset of the standards movement), researchers labeled it a "crazy quilt."[14] Teachers in California's more than one thousand districts often received instructional or other policy-related messages from their own school leaders, district leaders (in large districts, perhaps multiple leadership committees), school boards, county offices of education, the state department of education, and the state board of education. Other states were no different—authority over teaching and learning was incredibly diffuse, and what concrete guidance did exist rarely got all the way to the instructional core of teaching and learning. Much more often it was focused simply on what courses students should take.

Early standards advocates were also correct that curriculum materials were weak. For starters, they emphasized breadth at the expense of depth, covering dozens or hundreds of topics at a surface level and nothing at a deeper level. Scholars described a curriculum that was "addicted to coverage" or "a mile wide and an inch deep."[15] At the same time, the books were seen as highly redundant and repetitive—one analysis found that just 30–50 percent of elementary mathematics textbook content was typically "new" material that wasn't included in prior grades' texts.[16] The blame for the poor-quality curriculum materials was in part attributed to the decentralized curriculum authority in the United States—publishers writing books to reach the lowest common denominator because there was no agreed-upon set of content and skills students needed to master.

And of course, professional learning—both in-service and preservice—also had serious limitations. Professional learning opportunities were often of relatively short duration—a few hours to a few days—and often provided inadequate opportunity for follow-up.[17] They rarely engaged teachers in sustained, ongoing learning opportunities in real classroom situations.[18] And they rarely included any kind of serious evaluation, making it more difficult to learn what was working and why.[19]

WHAT'S WRONG IN THE STANDARDS-BASED REFORM THEORY OF CHANGE

With so much right about the theory, what's wrong with it? And why do I argue it hasn't worked out in practice? This will be the focus of chapters 3–5, but the simple answer is that the solution to the problems raised—starting with standards and reinforcing them through a few other relatively weak policy instruments, all of which depend on buy-in and action from fifty states and thirteen thousand school districts—is not nearly strong enough a lever to actually address the problems. Indeed, the policy theory of action makes little sense because once it identifies the sources of poor teaching and learning in US schools—structures, governance, conflicting guidance—it hardly tries to address those sources. Standards-based reform accepts that the structures of US education make direct reform challenging—politically and perhaps logistically as well—and rather than trying to change those structures, it just puts forth a policy approach that fits with current structures and hopes for the best. This approach—of ceding all of the important control that might actually lead to change—occurs throughout the theory, and the result is a reform that simply doesn't have the teeth it needs to accomplish what it wants, *especially* given that the structure remains so unbelievably decentralized.

To see this, return to the problems standards advocates identified and their proposed solutions. The question is how to get teachers to teach the content that we want them to teach—that we think is important for students to know. Essentially, there are three policy instruments proposed. The first is to try to convince teachers to teach the content in the standards through assessment and accountability. This approach is limited in several obvious ways. It assumes we have the testing technology to truly reinforce the standards and not undermine them. It assumes that the accountability incentives will be sharp enough that they will matter to teachers (motivating most or all of them to actually care about implementing them) and not so sharp that they will drive teachers out or produce other negative unintended consequences. And it assumes that teachers who are motivated to teach the standards will have or develop the capacity to do so. There are serious weaknesses in all of these assumptions.

The second policy instrument is to provide teachers with additional support through high-quality curriculum materials (though not to mandate any particular materials, because that's off the table). This approach, too, is limited. The most obvious limitation is that without any kind of requirement from the state, districts can and often do ignore curriculum recommendations.[20] Incentives, such as bulk discounts or eased administrative requirements, could induce more districts to sign on, but many will not—then what? A second obvious limitation is that adopting good materials is only half the battle, and maybe not even the hard half. Districts adopting good, standards-aligned materials still need to support or convince teachers to actually use them and use them in the ways intended by their authors. There is really nothing in the policy theory that can overcome this hurdle.

The third is to provide high-quality preservice and in-service professional learning opportunities. This approach is the weakest of them all. In terms of preservice training, the state has close to zero authority over preservice teacher education, and college professors aren't exactly known for responding intently to state policies or modifying their curriculum to suit external suggestions. In terms of in-service training, to get any kind of large-scale consistency there would need to be some state- or other high-level control, but there is little precedent or capacity at these levels to offer that control. And for either preservice or in-service teacher education, it's not clear what you'd actually want to be educating teachers about to get them to implement the standards better. Are you teaching them the content in the standards? Are you teaching them how students should be taught that content? Are you teaching them how to create or identify curricula to align with those standards? All of these are difficult and hard to imagine thirteen thousand individual districts doing well (or a state stepping up to deliver with any kind of consistency).

So, could it happen that standards implementation would go well? Could the theory of action play out close to how the policy makers and advocates envisioned? Maybe, but it doesn't seem very likely. Everything would have to go just right, really. The standards would have to be good. Teachers would have to want to teach them. There'd have to be good materials available, districts would have to choose them, and teachers would have to want to implement them. Teacher training would have to be strong, so teachers understood the standards and what they were supposed to be doing. And all of this would have to happen across fifty states and thousands of districts, and then persist across decades and through different administrations and leadership at the state and district levels. In short, the system is set up to thwart policy success. And as we will see in the next chapter, standards-based reform policy has not been very successful.

WHY HAVE STANDARDS FAILED? THE USUAL SUSPECTS AND SOME NEW ANSWERS

This book argues that, measured against its own goals, the standards movement is a failure. While standards-plus-accountability has boosted achievement a bit, these gains may have been somewhat illusory, and this reform has not led to appreciable gap closure.[21] Indeed, the magnitude of socioeconomic achievement gaps on national assessments is just as large in 2019 as it was in 2000. More importantly, there is no reason to believe that any tinkering with the policy—as the Every Student Succeeds Act aims to do—will make the law a success. Simply put, the idea of standards is poorly aligned with the goal of narrowing gaps, and the standards movement uses policy levers that are far too weak to actually achieve the kind of major instructional improvements needed to boost achievement and narrow gaps at scale.

A number of narratives have been offered for the failure of standards, and there is some truth to all of them. I discuss these arguments at length in the next chapter. This book argues that the "usual suspects" that are offered to explain the failure of standards are fine, to a point, but they are not the main reasons why standards have failed and will continue to fail. Standards are a failure first and foremost because they accept the flawed structures of American education as they are, rather than fundamentally challenging them. The standards movement recognizes the extreme decentralization of American education systems as a serious problem that gets in the way of meaningful improvement at scale. It rightly points out the ways that teachers receive conflicting messages—or sometimes no messages at all—about what they should be teaching and how. It correctly identifies the damning consequences of the (dis)organization of educational organizations, especially for the most disadvantaged students. But, rather than trying to fundamentally change this feature, the movement jerry-rigs a technical solution to the problem—it creates a set of standards and offers modest policy supports to get teachers to buy into and teach those standards.

The standards movement understands that teachers are the ground-level implementers with control over standards implementation, but it doesn't meaningfully grapple with the near-complete authority teachers have once the classroom door is shut. If we know now, and have known for fifty years, that teaching is an isolating profession defined by mostly individual practice, how can a light-touch reform like standards possibly penetrate the classroom in any meaningful way? If we know now, and have known for fifty years, that teachers almost universally choose to use their districts' formally adopted curriculum materials as one tool among many, why would we adopt a reform that is silent about supporting materials in ways that actually get them used? These decisions have doomed the policy to predictable failure.

Given this diagnosis, this book argues that focusing on technical fixes—improving the content of standards, tweaking the assessments, redesigning accountability systems—will not make standards work, because they are not the cause of standards' failure. In the final three chapters, the book offers an alternative approach that starts with high-quality, standardized curriculum materials and dramatic restructuring of educational authority. It argues that without a more radical reform that asserts greater state control over what materials teachers use and how they can be supported to use them, we may as well not bother trying to direct instruction through policy, as our decentralized structures are inherently unable to improve educational outcomes equitably. In short, the book argues that we have allowed local control to thwart educational improvement and we should stop doing that.

To make this argument, I rely both on reviews of what my and other scholars' research has found and on fresh empirical analyses using a variety of data sources. I describe these data sources in the data appendix, and I introduce them as they are used. This work spans the last half decade and includes both qualitative and quantitative research with a wide array of collaborators and students. The series of projects I report on began with a study of the alignment of widely used textbooks to the Common Core State Standards in the early years of the Common Core movement.[22] From there, and recognizing the growing evidence that curriculum materials might be an important tool for supporting teachers to implement the standards, I conducted a series of studies gathering data on the textbooks used in selected states across the nation.[23] That work also had a specific California focus, in light of a recent court case about the adequacy of curriculum materials in the state. I used the data I had collected on textbook adoptions in the state to randomly choose thirty-four districts to study. I interviewed district leaders to understand their textbook adoption policies and practices.[24] From there, I selected a sample of middle school mathematics teachers in each district and interviewed them about their involvement with the adoption, their implementation of the materials, and the supports they'd received from their district to implement the materials more faithfully. Next, I co-directed a national study of the implementation of college- and career-ready standards, and I co-led a project to conduct deep-dive case studies in five districts around the country focusing on standards implementation.[25] And finally, in the last few years I have joined research teams at RAND and Harvard to conduct and analyze state-representative surveys of both math and English language arts (ELA) teachers about their use of materials and the policy supports they receive.[26] I marshal these data throughout the rest of the book.

OUTLINE OF THE BOOK

The remainder of the book proceeds as follows. Chapter 2 reviews what we know about the implementation and impact of standards in America's schools. It argues that standards have not affected instruction to nearly the extent called for by their architects, and that the effects on student achievement have been modest and diminishing. It also argues that these effects have been no better for the disadvantaged student groups that need the most support. I end this chapter with a discussion of the popular explanations for the poor track record of the standards movement. In general, I conclude that existing claims have some truth to them, but that they are totally insufficient for explaining the ongoing failure of the standards movement.

Chapters 3, 4, and 5 offer explanations for why the standards movement has failed. Chapter 3 emphasizes structural issues in American education, specifically focusing on the remarkable decentralization and diffusion of authority that characterize our education systems. This chapter uses curriculum materials policies as a paradigmatic example of this decentralization and the ways that it results in poor-quality teaching and learning in American classrooms. It highlights, for instance, the diffusion of the textbook market, the relative lack of state involvement in local curriculum decisions, and the complicated processes by which districts make adoption decisions.

Chapter 4 focuses on the organization of American teaching and the ingrained cultural and structural barriers that impede large-scale instructional improvement. In short, this chapter asks what would happen if we could get quality materials in every classroom—would we see better teaching and learning? The chapter presents evidence that teachers have—and exercise—substantial control over their curricula. It also argues that this control is a central part of teachers' identity and is not meaningfully grappled with by the authors of standards-based reforms.

Chapter 5 focuses on key barriers to effective standards implementation in the area of instructional support for teachers and the coherence of state and district policy systems. In short, this chapter asks if we have the capacity in the system to train or work our way out of the problems identified in chapters 3 and 4. The chapter argues that standards are complicated and hard to understand in a consistent way and presents evidence that teachers often do not understand them in the ways intended by their authors. It also argues that teachers by and large do not teach in districts that provide them with coherent instructional systems to support their instruction and standards implementation. In short, it argues the capacity does not exist in our educational systems at present to deliver standards-aligned instruction at any kind of scale.

The final three chapters offer my thoughts on how we can actually achieve the goal set out by standards advocates—to improve instruction and student achievement at scale. The policy solutions are organized thematically and are arranged in order of increasing scope and ambition. Chapter 6 focuses on teacher-oriented strategies that are relatively feasible even given current systems. The main strategy emphasized here is to ensure all teachers have high-quality core curriculum materials and the supports they need to use those materials as much as possible and in the ways intended by their authors. In short, this chapter argues that only an approach that gets much closer to the classroom—which well-supported curriculum materials can do—has any hope of changing instruction across the system.

Chapter 7 focuses primarily on strategies that must be implemented by the state, including providing much more specific curriculum guidance, creating or adopting standards-aligned materials, and perhaps even mandating that districts adopt from a narrow list of approved materials. This chapter argues that states have the constitutional authority—and therefore, if they want to see real change, the obligation—to more tightly control and support curriculum. In exchange, teachers can reorient their instructional efforts around collaboration and differentiation, which they are better positioned to do than to evaluate and choose materials.

The final chapter gets around to the question of whether any policy can improve US schools at scale in the context of current governance structures. This chapter concludes that decentralization and local control are fundamental barriers to equity and excellence and proposes a more serious reenvisioning of educational structures with an orientation toward a new progressive vision for education. This chapter presents the boldest and most ambitious critique of our educational system, and it also highlights other interconnected social structures and problems that contribute to educational inequities.

THE GOAL OF THIS BOOK

Having introduced the structure of the book, I think it's important to take a step back and clarify what this book intends to accomplish and what principles it accepts as a given.

First, this book accepts the idea that educational reform must focus on instruction if the goal is to drive improvements in student outcomes. Research and theory make very clear that the teacher-student-curriculum relationship is at the absolute heart of what goes on in schools.[27] Further, there is compelling evidence that pedagogical quality and curriculum matter for student outcomes.[28] Indeed, this book takes the importance of curriculum materials and quality instruction as established facts—children will not learn more or better unless they are taught better.

Second, the book agrees that education policy—district, state, and federal—matters tremendously for improving education at scale. From civil rights to school finance, there are numerous examples of policies that have improved education. There is no reason that instructional policies can't also accomplish important change, even if it may be more difficult to achieve.

Third, this book views teachers as essential actors, not barriers to the implementation of effective instructional policy. To be sure, the book is quite critical of the policy makers who have designed instructional policies that cannot work in the confines of our educational systems and structure with the teachers we have now. Indeed, I recognize and call out the Herculean task we have given teachers over the last thirty years to read and interpret standards and select curriculum materials to align with those standards. Data make clear that teachers spend inordinate amounts of time and money selecting instructional materials, almost certainly to the detriment of both themselves and their students. The book argues for a course of policy that can ease teachers' workloads and enhance teacher professionalism while still improving instructional content and quality at scale.

What do I hope to accomplish in this book? This book is a synthesis of what we know about the implementation and effects of standards. This book is a data-driven critique of the design of standards policies and an argument about the ways instructional reform might succeed at scale. This book is a challenge to those who try to work through the system for reform and a call for greater effort to fundamentally rethink that system. This book presents an argument that hasn't been made: one that draws on lessons learned from decades of research on a movement that hasn't produced the kind of change we need to see. The standards movement represented the best-laid plans of well-intentioned policy makers and academics. It's gone awry, and now is the time to set the instructional reform agenda back on track.

CHAPTER 2

Thirty Years of Disappointment

As I argued in the previous chapter, the theories underlying standards-based reform are broadly correct in their diagnoses of the problems of instruction in American schools. But I also argued that the reforms proposed by proponents did not go nearly far enough in addressing the very diagnoses they identified.

Given this argument, we might expect the standards movement to have failed in implementation and impact in fairly predictable ways. For instance, we might expect that the key instructional supports called for in the theory (curriculum materials, assessments, professional learning) would not materialize, or they would be of insufficient quality or alignment. As a result, we might further expect that teachers' implementation of the standards would be weaker than hoped for. And in turn, we might predict that the achievement impacts of standards would be far less than predicted. In this chapter, I argue that all three of these predictions are accurate. Reviewing several decades of research on the implementation and effects of standards, I conclude that, while there have been occasional bright spots, the broad pattern is one of insufficient instructional support, modest instructional change, and inadequate improvements in student performance. Furthermore, there are troubling signs that what modest progress was made during the first phase of the standards movement has died out significantly in the most recent decade.

One challenge of the task of synthesizing the research on the impact of standards is that standards have rarely been a stand-alone reform. Almost always, they are packaged with some form of accountability assessment. Parsing the independent effects of standards, or arguing what the effects of standards would be in the absence of testing and accountability, is a very tall order. To the extent possible in this chapter I try to make clear what kinds of reforms are being evaluated in the articles I am discussing. Almost always, the results I discuss here are based on studies of standards-based accountability systems (i.e., policy systems where content standards are paired with standardized testing and school-level accountability policies). In fact, this might be considered the most basic form of standards policy, and the type against which other versions of standards policies should be compared.

HOW HAVE STANDARDS BEEN IMPLEMENTED? ARE STANDARDS AFFECTING WHAT TEACHERS TEACH?

The most basic question about standards-based reform is whether the standards have affected teachers' instruction. The major instructional goal of the standards is that teachers will implement them—that the enacted curriculum in the classroom will align with the intended curriculum as written in the standards. Evaluating whether this has happened is actually quite challenging. You can't simply ask someone "Is your instruction aligned to state standards?" because of course everyone knows that the policy expects teachers to align their instruction. Neither can you get a particularly good gauge of alignment from observing a few of a teacher's lessons—alignment is a property of a whole year's instruction, so the alignment of a few lessons could be misleading.[1] Despite these challenges, there are some reasonably strong studies that attempt to get a handle on how well aligned instruction is with standards. In my view, the takeaway from this literature is that standards are not generally affecting what teachers teach to nearly the extent that the reform demands. However, standards do clearly affect instruction in both desirable and undesirable ways.

The early evidence on alignment from the pre-NCLB era addressed the question of alignment from a few different angles. One approach was to ask teachers about their coverage of certain content strands that were more or less represented in the standards. For instance, studies in individual states asked teachers to what extent they were changing their instruction on "algebraic ideas," which was a strand that was emphasized in those states' standards.[2] While the results indicated that teachers were increasing coverage of focal topics as called for by the standards, the coarseness of these content strands makes it unclear whether alignment is actually increasing (i.e., a teacher could be increasing focus on algebraic ideas in general but not the specific algebraic ideas in the grade-level standards).

Qualitative work from this era certainly cast doubt on the validity of these survey findings. For instance, observations of instruction in some states revealed that teachers were often making limited instructional changes but simply adding test-preparation activities to "align" to standards.[3] At best, this is a very superficial form of alignment. Instructional responses that were actually in line with the intended policy effects were rare and were concentrated in the places with the most favorable conditions (i.e., material and financial resources, beliefs and dominant practices that were already in line with the reform). In another study, analyses of teacher assignments often demonstrated misalignment, even when those assignments were specifically chosen by teachers for their high alignment.[4] In short, the evidence from this pre-NCLB era indicated that standards had not gotten into the classroom much.

The most compelling evidence of the effect of standards on teachers' instructional alignment comes from large-scale survey studies of teachers' instruction, most of which were conducted during the NCLB era and since. There are a few ways researchers have gotten around the problem of self-reported measures of alignment. One way is to ask teachers what they are teaching and then compare that with what they "should" be teaching according to the standards. These kinds of measures have better validity, because the "right" answer to the survey question—what policy makers want teachers to be doing—is not so obvious.[5] I have conducted a number of studies using this approach, analyzing thousands of teacher surveys across grades and states, mostly collected during the main part of the NCLB era (2003–2009). Based on my research, I reached several clear conclusions.

First, I found that alignment of instruction to standards wasn't very high.[6] This approach reports alignment on a 0 to 1 scale, where 1 means 100 percent of the content the teachers report teaching is aligned with grade-level standards. In my study of about twenty-eight thousand teachers, the average alignment values were between .25 and .5 depending on subject and grade (higher in mathematics and ELA than in science). This means that about half to three quarters of what teachers said they were teaching was misaligned in some way. Usually, misaligned teaching was when teachers reported covering content that was found in earlier or later grades' standards. Of course, there are perfectly reasonable explanations for off-grade misalignment, the most obvious of which is that teachers may need to offer remedial or advanced content to meet students' needs. Still, this low overall level of alignment calls into question the theory by which standards are going to improve student outcomes through aligned teaching.

Second, and somewhat more optimistically, I found that alignment was generally increasing over the years of the study—the heart of the NCLB era, from about 2003 to 2009.[7] These increases were not large, but they were not trivial either—on average, in mathematics teachers' alignment increases were about 2 to 4 percentile points per year (meaning after five or six years teachers would have moved from the 50th to around the 70th percentile. The increases were somewhat smaller in ELA and science, but these were still promising signs. That said, alignment was so low to start that these increases would have to continue at the same rate for forty to fifty years in order to see full alignment to standards.

Third, I found that several characteristics of teachers and classrooms were associated with stronger implementation of standards in the classroom. For instance, in one study I found that teachers' instructional alignment to standards increased as they gained more classroom experience (up to a point—alignment was no better and perhaps a little worse for highly senior teachers than midcareer teachers).[8] This makes sense—we might expect new teachers to be focused on pressing issues like classroom management, but that alignment would increase quickly, as does teacher effectiveness, in teachers' first few years.[9] That study also found that teachers with more of various forms of subject-area training, such as content-related courses and degrees, practiced more aligned instruction, while teachers who taught more English language learners practiced less aligned instruction. Again, these findings are intuitive if you think that teachers with more content knowledge might understand the standards more clearly and therefore implement them more fully or if you think that focusing on a specific group with language needs might lead one to emphasize alignment less.

Fourth, I found that policy also seemed to increase the likelihood that standards would influence teachers' instruction, though only to a modest extent. In this study I related features of state policies to teachers' instructional alignment.[10] Here, I found moderate evidence that the coherence of state standards-based reform policy was related to teachers' alignment. That is, in places where the assessments were better aligned with the standards— where they better reinforced the content messages of the standards—teachers practiced more aligned instruction. There was also modest evidence in that study that the strength of accountability policies—the degree to which state policies emphasized rewards and sanctions of various kinds—predicted greater alignment to standards. If you recall the centrality of test-to-standards coherence and the use of accountability in the original theories, both of these findings were squarely in line with standards-based reform theory. Still, the associations here were relatively modest.

There are a number of other pieces of evidence that also support the conclusion that standards are not influencing instruction to the degree that the policy requires in order to work. For example, one study involved observations of a school district's curriculum committee to try to gauge the extent to which the committee was interpreting standards in line with what the authors intended. The author found that the committee often interpreted the language in the standards in ways that were likely not intended by the writers of the standards, leading them to adopt and adapt a mathematics textbook that was in some ways fundamentally at odds with the philosophy and content in the standards.[11] For instance, the state standards called for an increased emphasis on student reasoning, whereas the textbook was highly procedural and teacher-directed. District leaders did not notice these differences in the student skills that were expected or found ways to make the textbook content seemingly fit under the standards in spite of their fundamental disagreement.

Another study of teachers' instruction and districts' responses to standards policy found very limited evidence that the instruction teachers were implementing was in line with the expectations of the standards.[12] Only four teachers out of the twenty-five observed balanced procedural and conceptual knowledge in the ways spelled out in the standards, with most teachers leaning heavily toward one approach or the other, often on the basis of their prior practice and beliefs. This and other studies point out the difficulties of standards influencing practice and teachers' tendency to incorporate what's called for in new instructional reforms into existing practices and ways of thinking about instruction. Just as I modify the content of my teaching slowly over time and in ways that do not represent a radical departure from the kind of teaching I have always done, so K–12 teachers do the same.

Newer evidence—from the Common Core era—points to the continued challenges of standards implementation. Nationally representative surveys from RAND's American Teacher Panel offer several pieces of evidence that standards have penetrated the classroom to a far lesser extent than is desired. Teachers are unlikely to implement the standards as intended if they do not know the standards, and the RAND surveys found that most mathematics teachers did not successfully identify which of a given set of content standards were from the grade level that they taught.[13] Similarly, math teachers were given several sets of content standards and asked to order them from low grade to high, and about a quarter of teachers successfully did this. In ELA, teachers were asked whether their standards expected them to "select texts for individual students based on their reading level" versus use "complex texts that all students are required to read" (the latter is aligned with current state standards). Only about a quarter of teachers correctly identified the second of the two options as being more aligned. ELA teachers also overwhelmingly indicated that it was more aligned to standards to teach ELA around skills and strategies, rather than around texts, which again runs counter to what the standards are intended to encourage.

The RAND data were also useful because they allowed the investigation of changes over time in teachers' understanding of and implementation of standards. Though their panel allowed study over only a one- or two-year period (depending on the question) between 2015 and 2017, the results were not especially promising. On the measures mentioned in the previous paragraph—math teachers' knowledge of grade-level standards, ELA teachers' use of grade-level versus student-level texts—there were few if any increases across years. In some cases, the trends seemed to be operating in the opposite direction (for instance, compared with 2015, in 2017 more teachers thought that standards-aligned ELA instruction should focus first on skills).

In short, the evidence (both qualitative and quantitative) over almost three decades of standards-based reforms is that standards have not influenced teachers' instruction in the direction and magnitude called for by the policy. Standards are simply not being implemented as intended in the classroom. Certainly there are exceptions to this rule—you can walk into classrooms all around the country and see standards-aligned instruction. There are even whole states that seem to be seeing evidence of greater alignment (more on this in subsequent chapters). And many teachers, though not the majority, according to the RAND data, interpret standards in the ways intended by their authors. But this is not the norm. And what evidence there is that things are getting better is quite modest and suggests very slow progress. Why have these results been so disappointing? I will turn to this question after discussing the effects of standards-based reform on student performance.

HOW HAVE STANDARDS AFFECTED STUDENT OUTCOMES?

Given that standards haven't changed teachers' instruction as much as reformers hoped, you'd expect that the impacts on student outcomes would also be more muted than the movement's lofty goals. Answering this question turns out to be just as difficult as answering the question about teachers' instruction, for several reasons. First, it is difficult (or perhaps even impossible) to tease out the effects of standards alone on student achievement. Standards reforms are almost always paired with other simultaneous reforms—typically at a minimum testing and accountability reforms—so isolating the effect of standards is challenging. Indeed, only a few recent studies have even attempted to do so. And it's not even clear whether the impact of standards alone is a relevant question since that is almost never how they are implemented.

Second, and relatedly, there are a variety of methodological challenges that make estimating the impact of standards complicated.[14] For example, how do you decide when standards reforms begin? Is it when the legislature adopts the standards, when the tests roll out, or when schools start adopting curriculum materials? If every state has adopted standards—often at or near the same time—how do you create the kinds of comparison groups you need to reach valid conclusions? This latter issue is especially relevant for recent standards reforms like Common Core, where states generally formally adopted the standards on similar time lines.

Third, there is the issue of the outcome measure and its alignment to the standards in question. Suppose you study the impact of a standards reform by using a national assessment like the National Assessment of Educational Progress (NAEP) or the SAT. Well, it certainly could be the case that the standards reform might not emphasize the skills that are assessed, in which case your report of the impact on student knowledge will be erroneous. On the flip side, using a test that is highly aligned to the standards might result in inflated impact estimates that wouldn't have shown up on a more general measure. It's not at all obvious which of these answers would be the "right" one—do we want to know whether standards have affected student knowledge of what they've been taught, or do we want to know whether standards have affected a more general measure of their knowledge and skills?

With these caveats in mind, what do we know about the effects of standards on student outcomes? First, there is no question that the descriptive trends in test scores have been positive, or at least not negative, depending on grade and subject. Figures 2.1 and 2.2 show trends in NAEP scores over the period from 1990 to the present. In both mathematics and reading, the trends are positive overall, though much more so in mathematics than in reading. The increases are especially pronounced in the 1990s and 2000s and are certainly broadly suggestive that the standards movement has improved student outcomes. Analyses of similar data in other subjects do not suggest that the gains in mathematics and ELA performance have come at the expense of science, social studies, or other subjects.

The best efforts to isolate the effects of standards-based reforms rely on comparisons of states that adopted standards-based reforms at different times. The strongest of these studies use NAEP data and variation in pre-NCLB or post-NCLB accountability policies.[15] These studies do generally find positive impacts of standards-based accountability policies on student outcomes, with effects concentrated in the earlier grades (grade 4) and

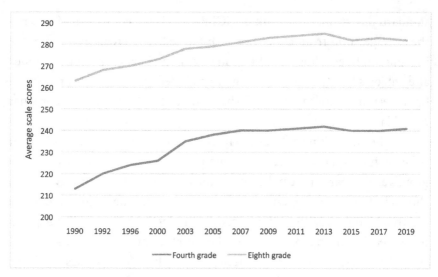

FIGURE 2.1. NAEP mathematics performance from 1990 to 2019.

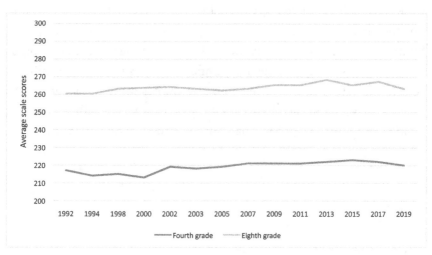

FIGURE 2.2. NAEP reading performance from 1992 to 2019.

in mathematics, though effects sometimes appear in ELA as well. However, the magnitude of these effects is almost always quite modest—certainly accounting for just a small portion of the large increases seen in the descriptive trend data. For instance, the best cited of these studies found an increase in fourth-grade mathematics achievement of about .23

standard deviations as a result of NCLB. This is the equivalent of moving the average child from about the 50th to the 59th percentile—not nothing, but not huge. However, this study found no increases in other grades and subjects.[16] Whether this is big or small depends on your perspective, but it certainly falls far short of what standards advocates hoped or what NCLB law demanded.

Another question that has been addressed is whether these kinds of reforms narrowed achievement gaps for children from disadvantaged groups as was part of the policy intention. Certainly the descriptive trends shown in figure 2.3 suggest that any gap closing has been quite modest— the trends look broadly similar between student groups, and the gaps do not appear much smaller now than they were when these reforms began.[17] Indeed, the research on this question generally finds very modest evidence of gap closing. For example, Dee and Jacob find evidence in some grades and subjects that lower-performing students and students from historically marginalized student groups gained more from NCLB, but they find no differences or even find widening of gaps in other grades and subjects.[18] Similarly, studies that have explicitly focused on the impact of accountability policies on achievement gaps find mixed results: accountability is seen to exacerbate gaps between high and low performers in some studies but modestly narrow racial-ethnic gaps in other studies.[19] Still, and clearly, looking at figure 2.3 lays bare that our outcome gaps remain large.

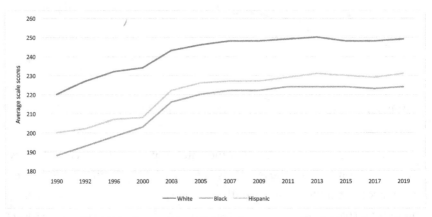

FIGURE 2.3.   Trends in the mathematics performance of racial/ethnic groups, from 1990 to 2019.

There are a few reasons to question whether these effects of standards-based accountability policies, which again are fairly modest, are really effects of standards or whether they are effects of accountability. One reason is because there are many studies that find positive effects of accountability policies that are not conflated with standards policies.[20] For example, there are a number of studies of school turnaround policies that offer schools the threat of closure or other sanctions, but not necessarily in the context of standards-based reform policies—these often show positive impacts even though they are rarely standards-oriented.[21] As another example, an early study in Texas compared schools in Dallas that were subject to accountability with schools in other large Texas cities that were not, finding large positive effects on test scores and other desired outcomes.[22] That accountability can boost performance without standards suggests that at least part of the standards-based reform impacts may be due to the accountability policies and not the standards per se.

Another reason to be skeptical that these effects are due mainly to the standards is because the one recent high-quality study that attempted to isolate the effects of standards from the effects of accountability found no evidence standards alone boosted student learning.[23] This study used methods and data similar to those used in the earlier studies of NCLB-era standards, but it was focused on the effects of "college- and career-ready" standards that have recently been adopted and implemented in the states. Thus, the time span under study was the last decade—about 2010 to the present. Not surprisingly, given the descriptive data shown in figures 2.1 and 2.2, this study found that student achievement stayed the same or went down with the implementation of these new college- and career-ready standards. It even found some evidence that the effects of new standards were becoming more negative over time. In other words, the single most direct piece of evidence about the impact of new standards is negative, again casting doubt on the role of the standards themselves in the standards-based reform impact.[24]

A third reason to be skeptical that these effects are mainly due to standards is because, as was discussed in the previous section, there is not much evidence that standards have been well implemented. It would be curious if a reform that only modestly affected classroom practice was responsible for substantial boosts in performance or narrowing of outcome gaps. It is as if your doctor told you to diet to lose weight, you did none of the things she suggested, and you lost weight anyway—would you attribute your weight loss to the actions you didn't take?

So what should be the takeaway from this research on the impacts of standards on student outcomes? I don't think there's any way to read the evidence and conclude the standards have harmed students—what evidence exists is overwhelmingly positive or neutral. Rather, I think the most reasonable summary of the evidence is that these reforms led to an initial bump in performance—perhaps as the worst curricula were refocused to the standards and improved in quality—but that the upward trajectory from this bump was not sustained. And indeed, there is some troubling evidence that trends are now pushing in the opposite direction, as performance has begun to dip in the last decade. Certainly there is not much room for optimism that trends will suddenly turn upward again. And even if we credit standards for all of the progress that has been made in the past few decades, this progress has been far less than was promised by standards advocates, and there has been very little evidence of performance gaps closing despite this having been pitched as an equity-oriented reform.

WHY HAVE STANDARDS FAILED? THE USUAL SUSPECTS

If we accept that the standards movement has failed, or at least that it has fallen far short of the goals it set for itself, why did this happen? In the rest of this chapter, I talk through some of the usual suspects that are blamed for weak implementation—and ultimately weak effects—of standards in the classroom.

The Tests

The commonly accepted wisdom is that state standardized tests are poor quality and are a major contributor to weak standards implementation. The argument typically emphasizes that state tests have primarily been multiple-choice because of the need to score large quantities of tests in a short amount of time and with minimal costs. As a result, these tests have been decried as "dumbed down."[25] Many have also argued that these assessments are poorly aligned to the standards they are intended to represent, and that this has contributed to teachers' poor implementation.[26] In short, teachers have focused on the tests because the tests are where the rubber hits the road. Since the tests are poor quality and poorly aligned to standards, teachers' instruction has been poor quality and poorly aligned to the standards.

The truth is that the quality of assessments has been a problem, though there are signs tests are somewhat better now than they were in prior decades. For example, I led a study that compared state tests with state standards in the NCLB era, and we found consistent problems with alignment.[27] Tests routinely failed to assess the more cognitively complex content in state standards, sending teachers the message that they should focus on more procedural or rote skills. Tests also sampled consistently and predictably from the standards, meaning they tended to repeatedly assess some areas of the standards and not others.[28] Again, this sends teachers the message that they should focus their efforts on the tested material—hence distorting their instruction toward the heavily emphasized, lower-level material.

There is some recent evidence that newer assessments are better than NCLB-era state tests along a number of dimensions. For example, the tests produced by two federally funded assessment consortia—Smarter Balanced and the Partnership for Assessment of Readiness for College and Careers (PARCC)—were found to contain more cognitively complex tasks, to require careful analysis of texts, and to focus on standards content to a greater extent than the "best-in-class" prior state test from Massachusetts.[29] And at least one state (New Hampshire) is experimenting with performance assessments, which engage students in far more authentic, real-world tasks (that are typically very expensive to create and score). In earlier generations of standards, some states did see positive instructional effects from these kinds of performance assessment reforms, though there were also a number of technical and cost-related difficulties.[30] Perhaps with new technology and thirty years of learning, there is reason to be optimistic that these more ambitious approaches to assessment could be an improvement.

While the tests do shoulder some of the blame for poor implementation, it is not as if there have been no advances in test development over the period of standards. Neither is it the case that states were forced to use poor-quality, mainly multiple-choice measures. That, so far into the standards movement, states continue to exercise poor judgment and choose cheap and dirty multiple-choice tests that undermine the standards, even caving to political pressure to drop consortium tests that showed real improvement, does not exactly inspire confidence that the tests will suddenly be getting better anytime soon.[31] So, yes, the tests are part of the problem, but we have known that for a very long time now, and relatively little has been done about it.

The Accountability Systems

Closely related to the tests are the accountability systems that are primarily used to hold schools accountable based on these test results. These systems have been criticized along a number of dimensions, but most notably for their overemphasis (or exclusive emphasis) on test scores, their focus on student achievement levels rather than student achievement growth, and their unreasonable and unattainable performance targets.[32] The argument goes that these design flaws reinforced the bad messages of the tests. The overemphasis on tests encouraged teachers to teach to the tests rather than the standards. The focus on student achievement levels meant the system disproportionately targeted schools serving low-income students. And the unreasonable performance targets meant the system encouraged reductive and sometimes perverse responses including massive cheating scandals.[33]

I have been a very vocal critic of the design of school accountability systems, so it goes without saying that I think there is some truth to this critique. From the standpoint of identifying schools that are effectively educating children, our accountability systems have been a mess. We have had the technology and the knowledge to design more thoughtful accountability systems for at least a decade, and scholars were well aware of the flaws of NCLB-era accountability systems from the earliest days of the law.[34] However, states were allowed to move away from NCLB-style accountability only recently, and even now most states maintain a moderate or strong reliance on the same kinds of performance measures and focus on tests (because the feds require this).[35] Still, there is enough variation in new accountability systems under the Every Student Succeeds Act that we may learn a bit about how to design accountability systems that don't undermine the intent of the standards.[36]

All that said, accountability systems bear relatively little burden in terms of their contribution to poor standards implementation. To be sure, the design of accountability systems does affect who feels pressure to respond to standards, but by all accounts in spite of the poor design almost all teachers feel that pressure. For instance, stress/pressure/burnout was the second most listed reason teachers considered leaving the profession on a recent national poll.[37] And test-focused accountability policies obviously result in teachers also focusing on the test, but that only really undermines standards implementation if the tests are not good (hence, I view this as more of a test problem than an accountability problem). So while I think we should set more attainable performance targets and we should refocus our accountability systems on identifying school effectiveness, those reforms will not meaningfully change standards implementation.

The Standards Themselves

Yet another common scapegoat for the failure of standards implementation is the standards themselves. The argument here is straightforward—standards are good and important, and if we had good standards they would be implemented. But we have bad standards in one way or another depending on who's analyzing them, and that's why standards implementation has been weak. Critiques of the standards from the NCLB era and from the Common Core era are many. For instance, one systematic review of all states' standards in the NCLB era found numerous weaknesses in both core subjects.[38] ELA standards were critiqued for (a) underemphasizing the role of content knowledge, (b) conflating literary and informational texts, (c) offering vague guidance for student writing, and (d) offering insufficient attention to a variety of genres, among other critiques. Math standards were critiqued for (a) underemphasizing arithmetic in the early grades, (b) avoiding specific guidance about the use of algorithms for operations, and (c) giving short shrift to fractions, among other critiques. Of course, other scholars criticized NCLB-era standards for different reasons, and there is no one right answer about what standards approach is "best."

Then of course there is the more general critique that NCLB-era standards were simply very different from one another, and that these state-to-state differences were hardly justified. In other words, math is math, whether you're in Texarkana, Texas, or Texarkana, Arkansas.[39] Furthermore, there is widespread belief, though perhaps not strong evidence, that the fifty-standards approach of the NCLB era undermined the quality of curriculum materials by forcing publishers to cram multiple states' content into each textbook. Common Core was intended to address these critiques of prior state standards, but there is far from universal agreement that the Common Core standards are strong.[40]

The Other Instructional Supports

Another common scapegoat for the failure of standards is lack of instructional support. Of the causes listed so far, this one probably has actually contributed the most to poor implementation. Usually, criticisms in this area refer to curriculum materials and professional learning opportunities, both preservice and in-service. The argument here is that teachers were not given sufficient, or sufficiently high-quality, instructional supports to understand and implement the standards. For curriculum materials, NCLB- and earlier-era curriculum materials were criticized along a number of dimensions. Detailed analyses from international comparative studies showed that US textbooks were far longer, covered far more topics, and emphasized procedural skills at the expense of skills demonstrating deeper understanding.[41] The precise source of these problems was not known, but these authors tended to blame in large part the same fragmented policy and governance systems that systemic reform advocates cited.

In the Common Core era, there is renewed emphasis on curriculum materials. And there have been some promising efforts to improve the quality of curriculum materials teachers have access to. The most notable such effort is EdReports.org, which offers reviews of popular curriculum materials against a rubric that includes dimensions of usability and Common Core alignment. But nine years into the Common Core experiment, these efforts to improve teachers' curriculum materials have shown remarkably little success. Early efforts to create Common Core–aligned textbooks were largely and accurately seen mostly as "slapping a new sticker on an old book," with studies indicating weak alignment to the standards themselves.[42] There haven't been updates to these early studies since the second wave of Common Core–aligned books came out, but EdReports does indicate that more and more commercially available books are meeting their standards for quality and alignment. Still, the proportion of teachers making use of "high-quality" materials is pretty low—only one of the top ten most-used mathematics textbooks according to recent RAND surveys was rated as meeting expectations by EdReports—and teachers are increasingly turning to supplemental and online materials of questionable quality.[43] To be sure, curriculum efforts like EngageNY have reached large numbers of classrooms, but most teachers today are still not using high-quality core curricula.[44] And those that are often use those materials only sporadically. If high-quality, aligned curriculum materials really are necessary to implement the standards, then this is indeed a likely contributor to poor implementation.

The same is true for professional learning opportunities, both preservice and in-service. We think we know what makes good in-service professional development—it has sufficient duration, it involves active learning and collective participation with colleagues, it is focused on content or the delivery of content, and so on—but surveys suggest this is not the kind of professional learning opportunities that teachers are often getting.[45] In a recent six-state survey of mathematics teachers, for instance, teachers reported receiving about two days of professional development that year on mathematics, and about three days total over their entire careers on their assigned mathematics textbook.[46] That same study found that only about two in five teachers were receiving any mathematics coaching, and that the average teacher met with their math coach just over one time per year. These are hardly amounts that suggest that teachers will have the opportunity to develop deep expertise in their curriculum or mathematics content.

Preservice teacher education is harder to study at any kind of scale, because our teacher preparation programs are, like everything in American education, unbelievably decentralized. There actually isn't very good evidence that teacher education programs differ much in terms of their effects on teachers' subsequent effectiveness.[47] That evidence notwithstanding, there have been some efforts to try to understand what is being taught in teacher education programs nationwide, and these efforts have been highly fraught and controversial.[48] Controversies aside, these reviews have suggested problems with the content delivered in our teacher education programs, again likely owing to the lack of efforts at higher levels (the states, federal authorities) to prescribe what goes on in teacher education programs. For instance, there is little standardization in terms of the content knowledge expectations in teacher education programs, nor is there much in the way of a content focus of any kind in elementary education programs. In short, while teacher education programs of course cover standards—what they are, how they should be implemented, and so forth—there is little evidence that they approach these topics in a way that would prepare most teachers to be ready to succeed at scale when they enter the classroom.

THE FAILURE OF THESE ARGUMENTS

Essentially, what these arguments boil down to is that standards could work if we just did them better. They're a great idea, they've just fallen down in implementation.

They would work if they were better quality and more clearly written, so teachers could understand and implement them as intended. But Common Core was supposed to do this, and many people believe the Common Core State Standards are high quality. And yet standards implementation lags.

They would work if the assessments were better quality and reinforced, rather than undermined, the standards. But indeed the new generation of assessments does improve on prior-generation tests along a number of dimensions. And yet states have backed off these higher-quality assessments, and standards implementation lags.

They would work if the accountability systems were better designed and sent clearer messages about which schools were in need of support and intervention. But indeed the new generation of accountability systems under the Every Student Succeeds Act moves away from a strict reliance on tests and largely rolls back the punitive consequences, instead focusing on diverse measures and student growth in many states. And yet standards implementation lags.

They would work if teachers had the curricular supports they need, and if they got the preservice and in-service support necessary to understand and implement the standards. But by all accounts there are many more high-quality materials available than ever before, and yet districts aren't adopting them and teachers are hardly using them. And we have a reasonably good sense of how to deliver effective professional learning opportunities, but this is not the kind of professional learning teachers say they get. So standards implementation lags.

In short, I argue that the popular explanations for the failure of the standards movement to achieve its intended goals are inadequate. The failure of standards to take hold is not about these technical issues. We can continue to improve the standards, tests, accountability systems, curriculum materials, and professional learning opportunities, but those improvements will not solve the fundamental failure of the reform to grapple with the real, underlying issues at play. We will waste more time, as more kids move through school systems that offer them inadequate curricula that fail to prepare them for success. In the next three chapters, I raise what I view to be the fundamental causes of the failure of standards. It is only by making the correct diagnosis of the problem that we can begin to solve it.

CHAPTER 3

The Case for Curriculum Materials

S ometimes it's worth reminding ourselves that the goal of the standards movement is consistency. Consistency in instruction across classrooms, across grades, across schools and districts. Consistency that ensures that all students receive instruction that is high quality and that prepares them for success in college and career. The standards movement clearly seeks to ensure consistency in what teachers teach and what students learn. And why is this goal so important? It's because lots of evidence suggests that students in the United States aren't learning as much as we'd like them to, and there are tremendous inequities in that learning. And, at least according to standards advocates, the incredible decentralization of our education systems and structures is one of the main barriers to improving teaching and learning at scale and offering equal opportunity to our students. This was the argument for standards thirty years ago, and not much has changed since then to undermine that argument.

This book is far from the first to point out that the US education system is, and has always been, incredibly decentralized. This is certainly true in terms of issues like school finance and more general issues of educational opportunity, where decentralization has perpetuated rampant inequities that have systematically harmed poor students and students of color.[1] But it is also true in issues of curriculum.[2] And while standards advocates correctly pointed out that decentralization was a barrier to improving instruction—and through it, opportunity—at scale, the reforms that have resulted have left the cause—decentralization—largely untouched.

This chapter highlights some of the ways that decentralization remains a barrier—the key barrier—to improving instruction at scale. It uses as an example the issue of curriculum materials. Curriculum materials, including (but not limited to) core textbooks, are one of the central policy instruments intended to support teachers' implementation of standards.[3] Indeed, they represent the very tools that are intended to help teachers bring the standards to life in the classroom. But it turns out that the decentralization of the American education system and the refusal of standards-based reformers to push for meaningful centralization and consistency through curriculum materials is a primary reason why teachers are not implementing standards. There is no consistency in the curriculum market at any level, and therefore there is limited consistency in what teachers are teaching (as we saw in the last chapter). Standards advocates thought that we could get good standards implementation without prescribing the curricula that make the standards real, but they were wrong.

THE MARKET FOR CURRICULUM MATERIALS

The first step in getting standards-aligned materials into teachers' hands is to create them and disseminate them through the marketplace. There is a perception among the public that the US textbook industry is dominated by the "Big Three" publishers—Pearson, Houghton Mifflin Harcourt, and McGraw Hill—and that these three publishers produce de facto standardization by virtue of creating the large majority of the materials that are actually used in teachers' classrooms.[4]

It is certainly true that there are three major publishers. It is also true that many schools and districts adopt materials produced by these publishers. But it is not true that there is anything close to a de facto standardized curriculum as a result. If anything, the evidence suggests that there are many players in the curriculum materials market—some big, some small. And the evidence also suggests that the concentration of the curriculum materials market has weakened over time. Indeed, there are more options than ever when it comes to schools' and districts' adoption decisions, and what's actually adopted seems to be becoming more diffuse as time goes on.[5]

Perhaps the clearest sign that there is no standardization in curriculum materials is that it's close to impossible to even get data on what materials are adopted and where they are used. Very few states keep track of these kinds of data, and those that do often do so in forms that are close to useless for understanding what's actually being used in schools.[6] However, what evidence exists suggests that far more than three materials are common, even within particular grades and subjects. For example, one state-representative six-state study of elementary mathematics recently found that there were thirty-eight different book series that district leaders reported using.[7] That's thirty-eight different ways of instantiating one set of standards.

To be sure, in that study the degree of concentration of the textbook market varied tremendously by state. In Louisiana, nearly 60 percent of schools used one material—Eureka Math/EngageNY (not published by one of the Big Three). In New Mexico, the top three materials accounted for 86.4 percent of the market (two of the three published by the Big Three). In contrast, markets like California and Maryland were much more diffuse. In these states, no one material had more than 18 percent market share. Data from teachers amplify this point. My own analysis of data from RAND's American Teacher Panel surveys in three states (Louisiana, Massachusetts, Rhode Island) focusing on high school ELA indicates that well over fifty distinct school-adopted core curricula are used by teachers in that subject and grade.[8]

The available materials certainly do not just come from large publishing houses, though many of the popular materials are indeed from the major publishers. For instance, in the six-state study of mathematics materials, the second most popular material was Eureka Math.[9] This is a published version of the EngageNY mathematics curriculum that was originally created by New York state under their Race to the Top grant, and it is published by Great Minds. Other non–Big Three book series among the most common in that study include Bridges in Mathematics (published by the Math Learning Center), Stepping Stones (published by ORIGO), and Ready Mathematics (published by Curriculum Associates).

Beyond the fact that there are large numbers of different materials available in the marketplace, the materials themselves differ in important ways (again undermining the idea that there is some kind of de facto national or even state curriculum from textbooks). Certainly one piece of evidence that core materials, from both major and minor publishers, differ substantially from one another is that expert reviews of their alignment and quality indicate as much. For example, EdReports is a nonprofit organization that provides ratings of the content and quality of core materials in the main subjects. In mathematics they have reviewed fifty-six textbook series, with just fourteen meeting all three of their standards.[10] In elementary ELA they have reviewed thirty-nine series, with just nineteen meeting all three standards. The other materials fall short in different ways—some for rigor, some for usability, and some for focus and coherence. Clearly, the expert reviewers of these materials think that they differ in meaningful ways.

In my own work, we have analyzed the content of dozens of elementary and middle school mathematics materials across two studies, and we have similarly concluded that they differ in important ways. For instance, one study of seven popular elementary mathematics textbooks used in Florida during the Common Core transition found that about two-thirds of the content of these textbooks was consistent from book to book.[11] While this is not a trivial degree of alignment, it also means that a third of the content of the materials was distinct, no small amount.

In an ongoing analysis of the most popular eighth-grade mathematics textbooks in California (again before and after the Common Core transition), we found that on average the books shared about 70 percent of their content in common, suggesting that there is still substantial uniqueness.[12] One way in which books in both studies differed from one another is in how much they emphasized advanced levels of cognitive demand—things like demonstrating understanding or applying methods to new contexts (the alternative being memorization or procedures). Textbooks sometimes differed by more than a factor of two in their level of emphasis on these advanced skills, and our more recent study suggests that there are systematic differences in the kinds of schools that adopt more and less cognitively demanding materials.

An example from two popular mathematics books illustrates these differences. One sixth-grade Common Core math standard is to "fluently add, subtract, multiply, and divide multi-digit decimals using the standard algorithm for each operation." This is a straightforward standard that is procedural in nature—students simply need to be able to perform the four mathematical procedures fluently. And indeed, this is how EngageNY approaches this standard—students are taught to take complex mixed numbers, turn them into decimals, and then carry out the operation as they would if these were whole numbers.[13] In contrast, Open Up Resources tackles this same standard in a far more conceptual way, using diagrams, web-based applets, and complex story problems, as well as demanding student explanation.[14] Both of these materials are rated as highly aligned by EdReports, but they could hardly be more different in how they approach this relatively straightforward standard. I would say the EngageNY approach represents a more literal read of the standards, but it's not at all obvious which of the two approaches is "best" from the standpoint of driving student mastery of the standards.

It is worth pausing for a moment here to highlight this issue, which represents a key weakness in the theory by which standards would lead to improved instruction at scale. Standards advocates intentionally and explicitly shied away from the issue of curriculum, leaving curriculum creation to the market and curriculum decisions to local control. What these data from teacher surveys and EdReports ratings lay bare is that this approach cannot work to achieve consistency in instruction across classrooms and schools. There are far too many different curricula being used, and those curricula are far too variable. Furthermore, many of the curricula that have been created and marketed to align to the standards simply do not do so. Getting standards implementation to the degree needed to see real instructional change under these circumstances is impossible. If we cannot even give school districts a small number of high-quality and well-aligned materials to choose from, we cannot achieve standards implementation.

In terms of both the materials available on the market and the content of the most popular materials, then, there is no reason to think that what's out there defines anything close to a de facto national curriculum. There isn't even a de facto state-level curriculum in any state, as far as I am aware.

There are simply too many books from too many publishers with too much different content for that claim to hold water. To be sure, standards-based reform advocates could have pushed, from the earliest days, for creation of one or a few sets of core materials that might have led toward greater consistency. For instance, the groups that funded the creation of the Common Core standards could subsequently and immediately have funded curriculum developers to create from-scratch materials to support the implementation of those standards. This would have accomplished several ends. First, it would have ensured (or at least dramatically increased the likelihood) that the materials created were meaningfully aligned to the standards. Second, it would have made these materials available much more rapidly than the market was able to produce otherwise—almost certainly they could have been widely available by 2012 (instead of 2014 and beyond, when most of the high-quality materials became available).

However, this kind of centralized curriculum development effort has very rarely happened. Indeed, standards writers have often gone to great lengths to emphasize that standards are not curriculum (see, for instance, the Common Core website, which repeatedly emphasizes that the standards "do not dictate curriculum").[15] Instead, the creation of standards-aligned materials has largely been left up to the market, and the results seem to be disappointing. Available materials are, on the whole, rated as poorly aligned with the content expectations of state standards.[16] Scholars have criticized the alignment and quality of textbooks in US schools for decades.[17] And district curriculum leaders have responded to these market failures by turning away from textbooks, even claiming "What we consider as a textbook is actually dead right now."[18] In short, this golden opportunity to support standards implementation at scale—by creating high-quality, aligned materials—has almost never come to pass because of fears about the control of curriculum.

THE STATE ROLE IN CURRICULUM

From 2017 to 2019, I did work with a state to help them think through strategies related to their department of education's role in curriculum adoption and implementation. The state leaders I worked with made it clear that they didn't know much at all about what curricula were being used in the state's districts, but that they wanted to know more. They also told me that they really would like to exercise more control over curriculum—at minimum providing districts some guidance about what materials were stronger or weaker—but that this was not the norm in this "local-control" state. And yet, when I proposed that they do just these things—begin to collect systematic data on what materials were being used in schools and districts around the state and conduct reviews to provide guidance to districts about what to adopt, these suggestions were immediately questioned for their feasibility. Requiring districts to tell the state what materials they adopted was seen as putting the camel's nose under the tent—these state leaders said that district folks would freak out and assume the state was trying to usurp their authority over teaching and learning.[19] Before I could even get to my more substantial recommendations, the state took this and other ideas that might meaningfully move the needle on curriculum completely off the table.

This example is not, I suspect, an aberration, and it represents a fundamental failure of the standards movement. The idea that states can achieve the goal of standards implementation at scale without even knowing what materials are being used in the public schools it operates is a farce. All states have the constitutional obligation to provide schooling to the children of their state. There is arguably nothing more central to the provision of education than the curriculum students are taught. The state seeks to shape that curriculum through the adoption of content standards. The state provides substantial educational dollars to local school districts—the majority in many states. And yet, in very few states does the state department of education offer anything more than advice to school districts about what materials they should use. In fact, in most states the state department of education doesn't even offer advice. The upshot is that in the vast majority of states, there is close to no meaningful state role in curriculum, and almost everything is left up to local actors.

Getting up-to-date information on state-level adoption policies is not easy—there is no definitive list available, and policies are changing all the time. At last count, something like twenty to twenty-five states (almost all in the South and West) practice some form of textbook adoption.[20] In the other twenty-five to thirty states, the state has no role at all in the adoption of textbooks or other curriculum materials. Despite the centrality of curriculum materials for influencing what and how teachers teach, these states are completely laissez-faire about what materials districts select, leaving the choice up to local districts without providing so much as a shred of guidance about the kinds of choices that would be better or worse.

Typically states that have anything to say about curriculum materials do advisory statewide adoptions. The state assembles a committee of educators and other experts; that committee reviews a large group of submitted materials, and then they put out a list of the materials that meet state expectations.[21] There is a long history of hand-wringing about states' roles in textbook adoption decisions. A great deal of ink was spilled in the 1980s and 1990s about the poor quality of state adoption processes and the negative impact of these processes on the content and quality of books.[22] Many of these critiques seem downright hackneyed by today's standards—for instance, the argument that smaller publishers cannot enter the market hardly holds up anymore when the majority of the mathematics and ELA materials approved by California are published by non–Big Three publishers. The argument that textbook adoption committees are inevitably politicized in negative ways is belied by the successful creation and dissemination of curricula by deep-blue New York and deep-red Louisiana. But more to the point, publishers are undoubtedly far savvier and more politically flexible than they were in the 1980s and can navigate potentially thorny politics of state adoptions with relatively modest modifications, if it comes to that.[23]

Perhaps as a result of these concerns about the quality of state adoptions, states that were historically proudly centralized in their authority over textbook adoption decisions (most notably California, Texas, and Florida) now allow districts to adopt whatever materials they want, on-list or off. Indeed (though, again, obtaining an exact count is difficult), I believe all states that put out adoption lists are advisory these days. At most, these states put forth modest incentives for districts to adopt from the state list, such as making purchasing of on-list materials easier by reducing red tape or offering reduced prices.

When states conduct their reviews and create their state-approved lists, they often use rubrics and committees of experienced educators to review and vet the proposed materials. Interestingly, though the review committees undoubtedly learn quite a lot about the quality of the materials they eventually do and do not adopt, this information is typically not made available to school districts. That is, rather than putting out the ratings of each of the materials they evaluate—the areas of strength and weakness, the committee's views on where and how the materials might be best used—the final list is typically just a list of textbook titles that are deemed "fully aligned."

In short, states have for the most part not done what they need to do to get standards-aligned curriculum materials adopted in schools and districts. They certainly haven't mandated any particular materials. In some states they have evaluated materials and made recommendations, but even these have been advisory. And when they have done these evaluations, they have done them in a way that makes them almost useless by refusing to provide detailed data about the strengths and weaknesses of the available materials. Even the most fundamental of state roles—tracking the educational opportunities provided in schools through the collection of textbook adoption data—is hardly practiced anywhere. It need not be this way. States do not have to—and they should not—give away their authority over curriculum materials and adoptions due to concerns about "local control."

THE LOUISIANA EXCEPTION

There is one prominent state that has been taking its role in curriculum much more seriously in recent years—Louisiana.[24] Recent and ongoing research makes clear that the state views curriculum as the linchpin in their instructional reform efforts. A careful study of Louisiana's approach offers ideas for how states can profitably involve themselves in supporting districts and educators to make better curriculum choices. And the research on Louisiana's efforts suggests that they are paying off in terms of teachers' instruction.

A 2016 analysis of Louisiana's strategy conducted by researchers at RAND found clear evidence that curriculum was an essential part of the state's reform agenda.[25] First, Louisiana rates available curriculum materials on a three-tier scale (Tier 1 = best) using clear rubrics. These rubrics involve examining the materials grade by grade along a number of dimensions that focus on coherence, alignment, and usability. But not only do they put out lists of rated materials (as do many states), they actually provide annotated rubrics that detail why they gave each material the rating they did. For instance, the rubric for Math Expressions, which was rated as a Tier 2 curriculum, noted as a weakness, "It is difficult to locate true examples of exercises focused on Math Practice 3 because a large number of lessons are connected to this Math Practice (e.g., In Unit 2, Math Practice 3 is linked to all 15 lessons)."[26] These detailed ratings make it much easier for districts to make informed adoption decisions, and they also provide districts with clear information about the weaknesses of the adopted materials that could inform their efforts to address those weaknesses.

Second, Louisiana rates a modest number of materials as Tier 1 and supports districts to choose Tier 1 materials (while still leaving the ultimate decision up to local districts). There are six elementary ELA and six elementary mathematics materials that are rated as Tier 1 materials, giving local districts a reasonable number of materials to evaluate and choose from. Interestingly, these materials are mostly not from the Big Three publishers. The state then supports districts to adopt Tier 1 materials through statewide contracts that make it easier for districts to procure them.

Third, the state actually developed materials when it identified that the market was not offering materials of sufficient quality for ELA grades 3–12. These Louisiana Guidebooks materials were developed because of this perceived market failure, and the state further supports their adoption by making most of the Guidebooks materials free to adopting districts. The Guidebooks, which are rated Tier 1, are now the most-used materials in the state.[27] The materials are also freely available on the state website, saving local districts money.

Fourth, the state supports teachers to learn about and better implement Tier 1 materials through professional development. For Tier 1 materials, the state provides a list of approved vendors who offer curriculum-specific professional development to support the materials. They also work with those vendors to ensure that a variety of packages are offered depending on districts' needs. And for certain materials, the state actually provides professional development directly to teacher leaders from Louisiana's school districts (there are approximately six thousand teacher leaders in the state, about three for every school), again with a focus on supporting the implementation of Tier 1 curricula. These teacher leaders are also involved in broader communication efforts from the state department of education to local school districts.

The state makes clear that it is not mandating that districts adopt any particular material or professional development provider: "We don't force anybody to purchase Tier 1 [professional development], but we only fund and endorse professional development providers that work with Tier 1 instruments. We will only do statewide contracts for bulk purchasing for Tier 1 contracts."[28] But by putting out detailed evaluations of core materials, facilitating their adoption through state contracts, and supporting implementation through either contracted or directly provided professional development, the state has encouraged districts to make adoption choices that align with the state's vision of instructional quality.

The result of these efforts is that districts have made those adoption choices, teachers are implementing the adopted materials, and teachers display higher knowledge about the standards than teachers in other states. For instance, on 2015 surveys from RAND, Louisiana teachers were twice as likely as teachers in other states to use EngageNY for mathematics and 60 percent more likely to use it for ELA. Louisiana ELA teachers were much less likely than teachers in other states to say that selecting texts for readers based on their individual reading levels was a strategy aligned with state standards (70 percent in other states, 47 percent in Louisiana) and were much more likely to say that skills should be taught through particular texts as well. Louisiana elementary math teachers were considerably more likely to correctly identify grade-level standards-aligned content than teachers elsewhere (57 percent versus 36 percent). And this knowledge spilled over into practice, with teachers more likely to report covering several standards-aligned ELA content areas than teachers in other states.

Recent interviews make clear that the state is continuing and even deepening this emphasis on Tier 1 curriculum materials. As part of a project on curriculum coherence in middle and high school ELA, we interviewed state leaders in 2018–19 about their ongoing initiatives in this area. Louisiana leaders reported several important trends and changes in curriculum-related policy. First, they were continuing to revise and improve their state-created Guidebooks curriculum in response to implementation feedback. For instance, they built out the initial version into a "Guidebooks 2.0" version that included more detailed lesson plans and assessment materials, and they recently completed a "Guidebooks 3.0" version that added supports for diverse learners. Second, the state continues to encourage districts to adopt Tier 1 materials by offering discounted state contracts and making Tier 1 adoption a condition of receiving certain state competitive grants. As a result, over 80 percent of schools have adopted Tier 1 curricula.[29] Third, the state has expanded its summer teacher leader professional development offerings. All Tier 1 curriculum publishers are invited to deliver statewide professional development to teacher leaders in these summer workshops, and Guidebooks in particular are supported with differentiated professional development offerings based on teacher leaders' experience with the curriculum. Fourth, the state has begun training content leaders in Guidebooks to return to districts and provide differentiated support on that curriculum.

Louisiana's efforts make clear that the state is taking seriously its role in ensuring effective standards implementation in the classroom in a way that no other state is doing. They are laying out a path that other states can follow and tailor to their own local politics. They are also demonstrating that effective standards implementation efforts need not be hemmed in by inadequacies in the curriculum market. More states should follow their ambitious lead.

DISTRICT TEXTBOOK ADOPTION

Once materials are created and adopted (or not) at the state level, schools and districts must make adoption decisions. Each of the more than thirteen thousand districts across the United States—not to mention individual charter schools and schools in nonuniform adopting districts—must establish a process for choosing the materials, evaluate the available options, and make a decision. In the states without even advisory state adoptions, this process has little to no guidance on which to draw (with EdReports being one high-profile exception). In principle, this process might have been made easier by the adoption of Common Core State Standards, because it allows for cross-state collaborations on textbook decisions. And it might also have evolved over time in positive directions, since districts in all states have now been making adoption decisions under multiple sets of standards for at least two decades. But even in advisory adoption states, this process is unnecessarily onerous and likely gets in the way of high-quality adoptions.

Not much is known about how districts make these decisions. Just one study had investigated this topic in any depth when my research team and I set out to study these adoption decisions in California districts post–Common Core. From 2015 to 2017 we interviewed district leaders in thirty-four California districts, which we chose to be representative in terms of size and student performance levels.[30] We also were sure to select districts that varied in terms of whether they had made adoption decisions recently and of what type. We chose some districts that had adopted materials from the state-approved list, some districts that had chosen off-list materials, some that hadn't yet made a decision, and some where we didn't know what kind of decision they'd made. We asked them about the role of the state-approved list, their other sources of information, and the process by which they made adoption decisions. Based on the interviews, we reached several conclusions.

First, most districts spend a lot of time and energy making adoption decisions. Typically, the process takes several months to one full academic year. In the districts we examined, the process is generally divided into roughly two phases. In the first phase, one or more people—usually district assistant superintendents with perhaps a small committee of teachers or content leaders—make a first pass through the available materials and select a small number to evaluate in more depth. If the state-approved list is used, it usually happens at this stage when district leaders make the first cut. In the second phase, districts evaluate the materials in various ways, often using rubrics or conducting pilots that vary in length (from a few weeks to a full semester) and spread (from a small group of teachers to a large group or all). Finally, districts make a decision, typically based on a vote of teachers on the adoption committee, and vet it through the school board (which is seen as a formality). In short, there is a great deal of effort that goes into choosing materials to adopt.

Second, districts use a variety of criteria to evaluate the available textbooks. Many districts use a tool kit that the state puts out in order to evaluate the materials. The tool kit lays out a number of dimensions on which the materials should be rated and proposes procedures for doing so (again, why the state doesn't also provide its own ratings, which were done using similar rubrics, is unclear). Some districts adopt the tool kit as written, others use modified versions created by California's county offices of education, and still others modify the tool kit themselves to focus only on certain dimensions.

Among districts that don't use the tool kit, many build their own measures. For instance, one district described evaluating each of three materials on five criteria: alignment with content standards; program organization; assessment; universal access to include English language learners, special education, and gifted and talented education; and instructional planning and support. The only district that did not use a rubric with multiple criteria to evaluate the materials was the smallest district in our sample, a rural district of fewer than two hundred students where the superintendent also served as a math teacher. As judged by these thirty-plus randomly chosen districts, the typical district in California evaluates multiple materials against multiple criteria, using an array of rubrics and measures.

Third, districts engage in strategic behaviors as pertains to the timing of textbook adoptions. Some districts reported that they felt intense pressure from their teachers in the early years of Common Core to adopt *something*, so they moved earlier than even the state-approved list. In these districts, they often expressed regret later on, because their adopted materials were seen as lower quality than materials created later in the Common Core era. Other districts took just the opposite approach, purposefully waiting to adopt. For instance, one district curriculum leader said:

> Then we have the ability to let a district adopt, and then talk to the teachers. Call 'em up on the phone say, "You've had it for the year, how did you like it?" Currently, we're looking at that with language arts, and everybody jumped into something called [textbook title], and now we're starting to see people wishing they'd got [a different textbook].

These leaders reported satisfaction with their decision to hold off on adoption, but in the interim there was a great deal of effort to offer teachers instructional support before a textbook was adopted. The timing of these adoption decisions undoubtedly has an impact on teachers' implementation of standards, both in the early years (before some districts have made an adoption decision) and in the later years (when some districts that adopted early are stuck with materials they feel are poor quality).

Fourth, a few districts—in our sample, just two of thirty-four—had opted out of the textbook market entirely and created their own in-house curriculum. Both of these districts were large (more than forty thousand students) and highly impoverished (80 percent or more receiving free or reduced-price lunch). In both districts, leaders expressed that the creation of in-house curriculum materials was a response to the perception that there were no good materials available in the early years of the Common Core period. Both also expressed that district leadership was the catalyst for the decision to create materials—the district superintendent came in, saw what was available, and instructed the curriculum leadership in the district to create materials instead. The process of creating the materials was onerous—in one district, two hundred of the district's eighteen hundred teachers were involved in the creation of the materials. The folks we interviewed expressed that they felt there was value in the process of creating materials, but also expressed some concerns. For instance, creating materials turned out not to be much less expensive than simply buying materials, because of all the teacher release time required. The in-house materials were seen as inadequately supportive by about half of teachers in one district, who wanted more day-to-day guidance than they received. And the materials were especially problematic for new teachers, who felt at sea without clear curriculum guidance. Interestingly, within two years after our interviews, both districts—feeling that the textbook market had improved, and under new leadership—adopted materials in the core subjects.

Our fifth observation was that, despite all this effort and rigmarole, what districts ended up adopting didn't really seem to be related in any systematic way to the processes they used or the criteria they said they considered. Two district leaders would say they used similar processes and criteria, but their adoption decisions would be opposite. Or a district leader would say that they waited until the quality in the market improved before making an adoption decision, but then they chose a material that was poorly rated by EdReports.

As best we could tell, the district adoption process mainly served two core functions. First, it gave the adoption the air of legitimacy. By going through the complicated process, including presenting the adopted materials for board approval, the perception was that the adopted materials were good. This symbolic function is important because some district leaders expressed limited faith in the state's statewide adoption process (e.g., they felt it was too shallow and not rigorous enough). Second, and depending heavily on the structure of the process, districts' adoption efforts increased teacher support for the adopted materials. In districts where teachers were heavily involved in the selection of materials, and where the ultimate decision seemed to come primarily from teachers, their support for the adopted materials was much stronger. However, district leaders expressed concern about the capacity of teachers to conduct these kinds of evaluations given all the other demands on their time. Regardless, there was widespread agreement that involving teachers in adoption led to stronger buy-in and, therefore, more complete implementation.

Overall, we came away from our study of district textbook adoptions thinking that there was a lot of work being done with very little to show for it. District textbook adoptions take a substantial amount of time and resources and duplicate work that has already been done or could easily be done at a higher, more centralized level. The process of piloting materials likely negatively impacts students (because of misalignment in piloted materials and the difficulty of learning and implementing two curricula in a short time period). And in the end, district leaders expressed substantial discontent about the materials they eventually chose.

OTHER OPPORTUNITIES IN DISTRICT ADOPTIONS

In our interviews with district leaders, we also uncovered several policy-relevant opportunities that point toward a desire for greater support from state authorities around curriculum adoption. First, there is some skepticism about the state's adoption process. In large part, this is because the items on the state-approved list are all viewed as flawed in one way or another. Thus, when the state says that certain materials meet an alignment threshold and are therefore approved but these materials still have clear weaknesses that emerge during district adoptions, this undermines district leaders' and teachers' faith in the quality of the state's evaluations. If instead the state provided their full reviews, pointing out the strengths and the weaknesses of the available materials, this could paradoxically increase educators' faith in the quality of those reviews and perhaps lead them to focus their efforts on remediating areas of need with the available materials.

The second opportunity we saw was for district collaboration around textbook adoption. In some of the small, rural districts, district leaders told us that they didn't feel they had the internal capacity to conduct quality reviews (given that there might be just a handful of teachers in a given grade across the whole district). This issue, coupled with high levels of interdistrict student mobility, led them to make countywide textbook adoptions. The county office of education played an important role, bringing publishers and available materials to the office, convening leaders from each district, guiding them through an adoption rubric, and helping them ultimately make a selection. Even in larger districts, leaders expressed interest in working together with leaders from other districts to make adoption decisions. We argued from these findings that the state could play more of a brokering role in helping districts make adoption decisions, working through county offices or some other structure to support collaboration.

GIVING UP ALL THE IMPORTANT GROUND

Standards advocates and state leaders have, for the most part, given up all of the most important ground on the issue of curriculum materials adoption. It has always been clear that curriculum materials are an important policy instrument for supporting standards implementation. But as soon as standards writers finish writing the standards, rather than creating quality curriculum materials to support them, they have ceded that ground to the publishers on fear they might be seen as usurping local control of curriculum.

Similarly, states surely know that they can support stronger standards implementation by directing (or at least offering guidance on) what materials districts should adopt. But zero or close to zero states actually tell districts what to do, and not even half offer meaningful guidance. In the absence of this guidance, district adoption practices are all over the map. District leaders want information about the quality of materials but they don't know where to find it. They expend hours and hours of teacher time evaluating materials that have already been evaluated by dozens of state-level committees. And in the end, it's not at all clear that districts make adoption decisions that are right for their teachers or their children. In short, the system just doesn't work to either produce the best materials or get them through the classroom door.

These failures are due to our acceptance of—and fealty to—the decentralized American education system. And these are far from the only examples. Our fetishization of local control means that we cannot address funding inequities that arise from the dependence of school funding formulas on local property taxes. It means that we allow white parents to secede from disadvantaged districts, walling their children off from integrated schools. It stymies our efforts to improve teacher quality and to distribute quality teachers more equitably. By refusing to meaningfully challenge the decentralized structures in our education systems, we ensure that change can happen only at the level of individual schools and districts. With one hundred thousand schools and thirteen thousand districts, this is no way to drive large-scale improvement.

CHAPTER 4

Curriculum Control in US Classrooms

S tates and districts implementing standards-based reforms have not done enough to solve the decentralization problem, leaving unscathed the very systems that block high-quality materials from getting into teachers' hands. But the failure of the reform goes even deeper into the instructional core. The standards movement has paid insufficient attention to the culture of American teaching—its history, its organization, and the needs and preferences of the millions of practitioners who fill its ranks. This lack of attention has resulted, first, in dramatically more responsibility being placed on teachers—the responsibility to learn about, understand, select materials for, and implement the standards in the classroom—and, second, in the failure to provide teachers with meaningful skills to carry out these new responsibilities. Beyond simply being onerous, the responsibility to deeply understand the standards and use that understanding to select curricular materials flies in the face of the goal of ensuring consistent, high-quality instruction and content across classrooms.

Any time we talk about what happens in classrooms, people on all sides get justifiably sensitive that we are either blaming, blame-shifting, or making excuses for one group or another. So before proceeding further I think it is important to say a few things at the outset. First, teaching is a very hard job. Students come into the classroom with vastly different abilities, experiences, and needs (both academic and nonacademic). Plus, they are humans, not robots—they have emotions, they have good and bad days, they experience the vast majority of their lives outside the school walls, and they don't all respond the same way to any given intervention. One of the main challenges of teaching is navigating all this variation. And that challenge is especially daunting because teachers have generally lacked the kind of specific, high-quality support they need to do their jobs as well as they want to. Perhaps in light of the difficulty of the job, teachers say they want a solid core curriculum. When I interviewed district leaders and teachers in thirty-four California districts, district leaders routinely told me that, especially in the early days of new standards, teachers were clamoring for quality materials. And not one teacher of the sixty-three I spoke to said they didn't want strong core curriculum materials. Even the ones who mostly left the materials on the shelf felt that having the reference was valuable for them.

Second, teachers are—or ought to be—professionals with autonomy and authority. This is important for many reasons, not the least of which is that no one will want to be a teacher if the job of being a teacher is one that lacks these key features. Compensation matters, too, and teachers are indeed underpaid in many places. But even great compensation cannot make up for poor working conditions and a lack of authority. Furthermore, teachers cannot be thought of—or the goal cannot be a world where they are—empty vessels through which curriculum policies are enacted in the classroom. That is both unrealistic and undesirable—they, too, are humans who do the best they can to provide education to America's diverse (and increasingly underserved) student population. Treating teachers as cogs in a machine is a recipe for discontent and disaster.

With these views clearly stated, I argue that structural and organizational issues in American teaching are major barriers to both standards implementation and instructional improvement at scale. These issues have deep historical roots and cannot be papered over with a light-touch reform like standards.

THE STRUCTURE OF TEACHING

There is a long line of research in the sociology of teaching, perhaps the seminal work of which is Dan C. Lortie's 1975 book *Schoolteacher*.[1] This book lays out some of the key features of the teaching profession in the United States, many of which are relevant to the discussion of why standards have failed and why, even with high-quality and aligned curriculum materials, we may not see strong standards implementation.

History matters. The history of teaching, like that of any occupation, has shaped the profession. Lortie's book argues that one of the defining traits of American teaching is the "cellular" structure, where schools were explicitly designed for teacher separation rather than teacher cooperation and collegiality (a related term is the "egg crate" model of teaching).[2] This was done, he argues, to facilitate high turnover—because of teaching's rules (e.g., no married women can teach), a structure was needed that would allow schools to continue operating as normal even when there was high turnover. Similarly, teaching is structured as a "career-less" career, with teachers seeing little to no career advancement and pay structures that have nothing to do with performance or merit (typically rewarding only longevity and levels of education).[3] This can affect who is interested in teaching (people for whom career advancement and financial reward are not major drivers) and who stays in the profession over time. The structure of preservice professional learning is itself wildly decentralized, with few common expectations across programs and widespread criticism of its overly theoretical and unhelpful nature (the reason that most of teachers' actual learning takes place on the job).[4] It is worth noting that this last feature—the lack of connection between training and the actual job—is itself a knock-on effect of the decentralization discussed in the previous chapter. After all, how can we prepare teachers for success in a particular setting with particular students or a particular curriculum when we have no idea where they'll go or who or what they'll teach?

To this day, these structural features profoundly shape everything about teaching. Structures affect who decides to become a teacher (often those who did well in school themselves and therefore generally support its structures and systems).[5] Structures affect the nature of feedback and support that teachers receive—consider that teaching is an uncertain profession, and that the outcomes that teachers care about (student learning, but also socialization, creating lifelong learners, etc.) are difficult to measure even in the short term and all but impossible in the long term.[6] Even in the new era of annual teacher evaluation, teachers rarely receive the kind of models of good practice or feedback about their performance that many other professionals do.[7]

HOW MUCH CURRICULUM CONTROL DO TEACHERS HAVE?

How do we see these features manifesting with respect to standards and curriculum implementation? Based on rigorous qualitative and quantitative evidence, it is readily apparent that teachers have substantial autonomy over the instructional decisions inside their classroom walls. Indeed, classroom instructional decisions are the single area of authority where teachers have the most say.

First, district leaders make clear that they often leave things up to teachers when it comes to important curricular decisions. We surveyed district leaders in three states—Louisiana (a high-control state), Rhode Island, and Massachusetts—about their middle school and high school ELA teachers' curriculum use.[8] Of the 209 districts represented in our survey, more than half (56 percent) did not report that they required *any* curriculum materials for their middle school ELA teachers (an additional 6 percent said they didn't require any materials but did recommend some). In high school it was even rarer to require or recommend materials—just 34 percent of district leaders reported doing so. To be sure, curriculum materials adoption patterns vary across subjects and grades (higher in mathematics and science), but still large majorities of teachers are not assigned to implement any particular curriculum materials in their classes.

Second, teachers themselves say they have a good deal of control over many core instructional decisions. When Richard M. Ingersoll analyzed data from the nationally representative Schools and Staffing Survey (SASS) in the pre-NCLB era, large majorities of teachers (approximately two-thirds) said they had a "great deal of influence" over major instructional decisions like classroom teaching techniques and homework levels.[9] And while you might think that accountability-oriented reforms that have dominated the last two decades would have negatively affected teachers' perceptions of classroom control, this is not true. Research tracking responses to the SASS have found that, if anything, teachers' feelings of classroom control have *increased* over time by a nontrivial margin.[10] When we talked to California middle school math teachers about their curriculum and instruction post-Common Core, we virtually never heard indications that their instructional authority was being managed in any way. Even in the relatively rare cases in which districts and schools would provide teachers with reasonably specific instructional guidance (e.g., through a pacing guide), the teachers we spoke with felt totally free to follow that guidance or not. When it comes to what goes on inside the classroom walls, the teacher reigns.

Third, teachers demonstrate the control that they have through their instructional decision-making. The clearest example of this is the extent to which teachers report supplementing their schools' or districts' formally adopted curriculum materials.[11] Recent survey data from a variety of sources demonstrate this sharply. For just a few examples:

- A nationally representative survey study from RAND found that 88 percent of teachers reported that they used digital instructional materials during classroom instruction, with the large majority of these being supplemental uses (i.e., in addition to a core material they used more frequently).[12]
- Another national RAND survey found that 95 percent of elementary and 97 percent of secondary teachers reported using Google to find instructional materials.[13] In searching for materials to plan instruction and in delivering instruction in the classroom, teachers reported consulting a wide range of different resources.
- Elementary mathematics teachers in a six-state survey reported that they used teacher-created materials in 30 percent of all lessons, and these proportions are even higher in other subjects and grades.[14]

Beyond just supplementation, teachers also extensively modify their formally adopted materials. Figure 4.1 shows the frequency with which teachers report modifying their main curriculum materials each week (from a list of nine possible modifications like skipping or modifying activities because they are too easy for their students, adding enrichment activities to challenge students more, or modifying activities to better address the learning objectives or target standards). As seen in the graph, virtually all teachers modify their materials at least somewhat, and the average teacher reports making 13.5 modifications per week to their main instructional materials. The most frequent form of modification teachers reported was to add remediation (82 percent of teachers reported modifying their materials at least once a week for this purpose), but regardless of the nature of the modification, it is clear that teachers feel more than free to modify their core materials in whatever way suits their needs. In short, teachers have and exercise a great deal of control over their curriculum and instruction, even in instances where the school or district has adopted a core curriculum for them to use.

Fourth, teachers will gladly tell you about their curriculum implementation and supplementation patterns, and what they say is quite revealing. In our study of sixty-three eighth-grade mathematics teachers across more than thirty California districts, for instance, we found zero teachers—not one—who reported relying exclusively on district-adopted materials. We heard a variety of rationales and explanations for teachers' implementation

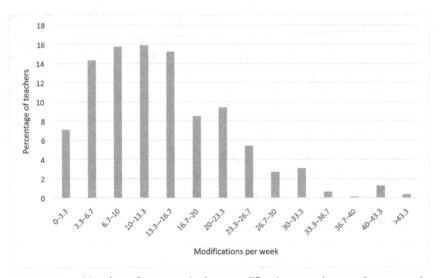

FIGURE 4.1.   Number of core curriculum modifications teachers make per week.

and supplementation decisions. One teacher who said she supplemented a good deal said, "Creating it ourselves, we know exactly what we're trying to get across... I feel pretty confident teaching a lesson I've created versus going off of one that's given to me that I might not necessarily understand the point of what they're wanting the students to do and why." Another teacher blamed textbook publishers for teachers' supplementation decisions: "The first few versions of the publishers' books looked just like—we literally turned it page for page... Side by side, we were like, 'all they did was name it Common Core and find the standard to match it.'" A third teacher emphasized the breadth of the standards versus the narrowness of the curriculum: "Within a standard, as you're probably familiar with, the standards can be quite broad. In many cases, the textbook doesn't seem to address all the aspects of a given standard so that you either have to provide supplementary materials or just do it out of direct instruction and get modeling to get the material across."

We heard other reasons as well. Teachers described textbooks as a "starting point"—the implication being that any material cannot be expected to provide all the content needed to get through the standards in a given year. Teachers described trusting the online curriculum materials from Teachers Pay Teachers and other websites because they were created by other teachers, rather than by publishers (though teachers also often modify even the supplemental materials they download).[15] Teachers described wanting materials that were more "familiar" or "normal," with one teacher collecting discarded textbooks from other schools and districts in the area and using them because "the older textbooks were more simple in the way they described things."

The point of this is not to enumerate every reason why teachers exercise their curricular autonomy in the classroom—there are too many reasons, and every teacher has her own reasons for doing so. Perhaps the most common reason that we have found in our research is to increase student engagement, but alignment, cultural relevance, perceived level of difficulty, and usability are also all common reasons.[16] Instead, the point is to argue that teachers are subject to very little curriculum control in US schools. And while aspects of teaching have changed during the standards and accountability era, teachers' ability to control their curriculum—to select and implement instructional materials they choose—remains a central, defining characteristic of American education. That was true before standards, and it's true now. Even when teachers are starting with the same core materials, what is actually enacted in the classroom ends up being remarkably different from classroom to classroom.

Not only do teachers have and exercise curriculum control in their classrooms, but this is a core part of their identity as teachers. This control connects back to the structural and historical issues raised by Lortie. For example, the cellular nature of teaching, with schools designed for teacher separation, facilitates an approach to instruction that leaves the individual teacher in charge. The lack of structured time in the schedule for collaboration further results in teachers being on their own when it comes to implementing or modifying adopted materials. The fact that those who select into teaching are those who enjoyed and did well in traditional classrooms themselves reinforces the approach that core curriculum materials are one tool among many (as that is what they experienced in classrooms when they were students). Whipsawing curricular fads—from phonics to whole language and back again—encourage frustrated teachers to stick to what they know and minimize their effort to understand and implement new materials. The difficulty of observing long-term outcomes that teachers care about may lead them to prioritize instructional materials that seem to affect student motivation and engagement in the short term, which they believe supplemental materials do.

The upshot of these data is that teachers are leery of, and resistant to, what may be perceived as top-down curriculum control. Take teachers' curriculum authority away, or enact policies that seem as if they might encroach on teachers' authority in that area, and teachers may feel they have no control left over their work. So instead of saying to teachers, "these are good materials for helping you teach the standards; we expect you to use them as the core of your curriculum most of the time," we get at best half measures—adopted materials that sit in the back of the room for show and are modified or supplemented when they are used at all. This is no path to curriculum coherence or standards implementation at scale, and it was always obvious that this would be the outcome in a system where the teacher controls the curriculum.

THE ALIGNMENT TRAP

To be sure, the standards movement could have tried to change teachers' curriculum authority, but it did not. Just as the standards movement hardly pushed at all on states' and districts' curriculum decisions, so too did it leave teachers' curriculum authority unscathed. And thanks to the internet, there are now more options available for teachers to use for supplementation than ever before. Of course, there are cases of individual schools and districts where scripted curriculum took hold, but the best research makes clear that this was not true on average during the NCLB era and it is certainly not true on average today.[17]

If anything, the standards movement placed new, different, and problematic forms of authority and responsibility on individual teachers, especially the responsibility to become alignment experts. Unlike many other dimensions by which we might evaluate some particular materials—quality, engagement, or organization, for example—alignment is an objective measure. Whether a book or a test is aligned to standards is a property of the book or test that we can measure; it is not a function of the students in the room or any individual's opinion. There are several established procedures for measuring alignment, and while none is considered the single gold standard, these procedures have been widely used and refined by experts for two decades.[18] These methods typically involve content experts and test developers who receive multiple-day trainings and conduct alignment analyses for multiple states. They require a deep knowledge of the standards and often of complex content frameworks that contains hundreds of topics and multiple levels of cognitive demand. This is arduous work.

To be sure, we could train teachers to use these methods—it is certainly within their capacity to do this kind of work. But we have not, and just a little thought makes it clear that training millions of teachers and having individual districts, schools, or teachers evaluate and adjudicate alignment decisions—or construct their own aligned curricula—makes no sense. If alignment is a property of a material as compared with a target, why should individual teachers be evaluating alignment as part of district alignment committees? Their answers should always be the same (at least in states with the same standards), so the exercise would just be one that takes a lot of time and introduces a lot of noise into the alignment decision. Similarly, why should individual teachers be evaluating their districts' adopted materials to determine alignment, seek out supplemental materials to address alignment problems, or identify aligned materials from among the sea of resources online? Again, the materials (core materials or supplementary materials) are aligned or they're not aligned—this is a property of the materials themselves, not a teacher's opinion.

That said, measuring alignment is quite difficult and labor-intensive. We might like to think that spotting alignment is (to paraphrase Supreme Court Justice Potter Stewart) like spotting obscenity—you know it when you see it. But it's not. Whether you're using either of the two most common alignment approaches from research, or whether you're using the rubrics and tools from EdReports.org, becoming an expert in alignment—how to measure it and how to identify gaps in alignment—requires substantial training and expertise. Teachers by and large do not receive training on alignment even approaching what EdReports reviewers do, so why would we expect them to develop that expertise?

Indeed, there is compelling evidence teachers are not alignment experts. From 2015 to 2017, my research team and I conducted interviews with school district leaders and randomly chosen eighth-grade mathematics teachers from across thirty-four randomly chosen California districts (with the intention of being representative of teachers in the state).[19] In total, we spoke with thirty-four districts' leaders and sixty-three teachers. We asked these teachers about a range of topics, including about their schools' formally adopted curriculum materials and whether they were aligned to standards. Of the teachers who had an opinion on this question (about 20 percent said they couldn't answer but assumed so because the materials were adopted by their district), over 90 percent said their materials were indeed aligned with state standards. But many of the materials they claimed as aligned are actually rated as not aligned by EdReports—Big Ideas, Go Math!, Springboard, Carnegie—many of the most-used materials across the state.

Even at the level of the individual objective, the issue of standards alignment looms large in terms of what we expect teachers to be doing under the standards regime. Typically, teachers are taught in their teacher education programs to identify the objective or objectives of each lesson, perhaps even to write that objective on the board. Then they are taught to design or select the lesson around that objective. This piecemeal approach requires teachers to parse the wording of individual objectives, to identify or create resources for those objectives, to determine appropriate sequencing of material, and so on. But even at the level of the individual objective, alignment should be thought of as a measurable property of a lesson relative to an instructional target (not to mention that it is much more productive to think of a curriculum as a coherent set of activities that, together, embody the standards). It makes little sense for teachers to spend precious time deciding what materials are and are not aligned to an individual objective when they have little training or expertise in how to do so. And even if we could train them well, if alignment is an objective property and not a function of the teacher's views or the students in the classroom, why should individuals be rating alignment? The answer is that they shouldn't—alignment should be a focus of curriculum and test writers, and the focus for teachers should be on implementing, seeing what works well and what does not, and shoring up areas of weakness.

In short, the way standards have been interpreted and implemented from the state level on down, teachers are now expected to use their expertise to, first, read and understand the standards and, second, ensure the curriculum materials they choose and enact are aligned with those standards. This is a whole new expectation that simply didn't exist prior to standards-based reform that gets us things like teachers writing their objectives on the whiteboard for each lesson, lesson sharing websites tagging lessons with dozens of Common Core standards and letting teachers search and sort by standard, and school districts assembling committees of teachers to pore over textbooks and evaluate their alignment rather than relying on state alignment ratings. These are new expectations, and they are onerous and difficult. And having teachers in every district do them is inefficient and wasteful of teachers' time. Putting teachers at the front lines of alignment makes little sense, and data back this conclusion up.

To be sure, while I do not think individual teachers should be spending their time internalizing standards and adjudicating the alignment of particular materials, reducing teacher discretion in this one area need not affect teacher control in other instructional areas. Teachers will always need to be able to modify materials during implementation to meet the needs of their students. Similarly, teachers will always have their own instructional styles and preferred approaches for implementing materials. Removing a burdensome expectation like alignment verification frees teachers up to work collaboratively with colleagues on implementing and supplementing materials that experts have determined are, at their core, high quality and well aligned with the instructional target.

NO CURRICULUM IS PERFECT

Talk to teachers about their students or their curriculum materials, and you are likely to get a range of answers with a consistent theme: there is no one set of materials that can work for their students because their students are too different (both from each other and often from other students in the school or district). For instance, I led a study where we examined the quality of the most-downloaded high school ELA materials on the top lesson-sharing websites and also interviewed a small sample of teachers about their use of these materials. The teachers we talked to told us that they go to these sites because "I'm always looking at college-level and middle-school-level materials to reach my higher and lower students" or "I have a set of three units, and they are amazing. Even so, I still need activities to go with these units because I might need multiple ways to reach certain students."[20]

In our larger study of teachers' implementation of the Common Core in the context of middle school mathematics, we heard this refrain over and over again in interviews with teachers—that the adopted curriculum, or even any curriculum at all, was inappropriate for some or all of their students. In fact, we heard a claim like this in the clear majority of the teacher interviews we conducted. Teachers expressed a variety of concerns about the appropriateness of their materials for their students. Some teachers had large proportions of English language learners and expressed that the English language demands of their materials were inappropriate for their students. Others noted that they had low or high achievers in their classes (or both!) and that the adopted materials were inappropriately challenging or easy for their students. So they would go to websites or old textbooks in the back of the classroom to address the perceived weaknesses of the materials they were supposed to be using.

There were several takeaways from these discussions with teachers about the appropriateness of curriculum materials for teachers' classes. One was that essentially every teacher thinks their formally adopted materials are inappropriate for at least some of their students (and possibly all of them). Another was that teachers' views about the appropriateness of their materials did seem to be related to the materials themselves (i.e., some materials were consistently described as "too easy" or "too hard" or "not engaging enough"), but they also seemed to be about the teachers' attitudes toward curriculum materials generally. We could see this because some teachers made it clear that they thought their job was to implement the materials they were given (even if they hated them, which we sometimes heard) while others in the same district would report implementing them much more loosely. We also see evidence from surveys that teachers vary in their views of textbooks—a recent study found that of the top seven most commonly used math textbooks, teachers were more than twice as likely to say EngageNY was too hard as compared with My Math, while My Math users were three times more likely to say their book was too easy).[21]

A third was that even when teachers in the same district had similar concerns about their adopted material, they would often supplement independently rather than collaboratively. One teacher would rely on the previous textbook they had used, while another would print out worksheets from a website. One teacher would build in projects they had written, while another would have students work through the technology component of their digital materials. There were some exceptions to this pattern—in districts and schools that had established clear structures, ample time, and expectations for teachers to be collaborating around curriculum implementation—but these exceptions were rare.

My research team and I came away from these interviews with a number of thoughts. First, we came away thinking that most teachers—again, nearly all in our data—were spending a lot of time and effort shoring up their curriculum materials because of perceived weaknesses. Survey data support that the search for quality curriculum materials is a major source of teacher effort. A nationally representative survey from RAND found that just under half of teachers (46 percent) reported spending more than four hours per week developing or selecting their own curriculum materials.[22] Some teachers spend even more time on this task—according to one study, teachers spend up to twelve hours a week searching for, selecting, modifying, and creating curriculum materials.[23]

Second, some teachers seemed to relish the task of supplementation, preferring to choose their own materials rather than implement what they were given. This was a small proportion of teachers overall—certainly far from a majority. But the teachers we talked to overwhelmingly stated that they wanted to have a good core curriculum as a backbone. Many of them even expressed resentment about the early years of Common Core, when they did not feel they had the resources they needed to implement the standards. And district leaders confirmed these findings, emphasizing how teachers needed curriculum support, especially in the early years of standards implementation, and that the available materials at the time simply didn't offer what was needed.

Third, schools and districts seemed to be missing opportunities to support teachers to supplement their materials in ways likely to improve their quality. For instance, while the most common refrain was that schools' adopted curriculum materials lacked sufficient opportunities for students to practice procedural skills (requiring teachers to turn to online or old materials to provide that practice), we did not hear examples of schools or districts attempting to fill this gap for teachers. Rather, we heard an "every teacher for herself" mentality that left teachers to their own devices and resulted in some teachers pulling from other curricula they had bought or found (e.g., EngageNY, other new textbooks, or old editions of textbooks), while others created or downloaded worksheets from a variety of websites, all to accomplish the same goal—providing students more practice. This is again a structural failure of a system that treats teachers as sole practitioners rather than members of an organized practice.

Of course, there is more than a kernel of truth to the idea that classrooms are unique, and therefore that teachers need to do some modification of whatever curriculum is formally adopted. Books also are imperfect and imperfectly matched to classrooms—some are too hard, others too easy; some are too conceptual, others too procedural—and whether a given book is one or the other depends to some extent on the students in the classroom. The solution to these facts has historically been that teachers have deputized themselves (or been granted the authority) to modify and supplement as they see fit.

But this approach isn't working. It's onerous for teachers. It leads to unacceptable variation in student opportunity (especially when we know that disadvantaged students most often get the least-experienced, least-qualified teachers on average). It also leads to the stories you hear about on social media like clockwork every fall and spring—teachers choosing wildly inappropriate supplemental materials from some website and implementing them to parents' horror.[24] We must not tell teachers to just implement books they know are inappropriate for their students, but neither should we assume that whatever they are supplementing with is better than what they are replacing. Rather, we must create structures that support teachers to work together to supplement and modify in ways that build coherence and quality and ensure curricular equity rather than undermine those goals.

We must also work to improve core materials over time so that teachers feel the need to supplement less and supplement in more quality-controlled ways. Of course we cannot know for sure that improving the core materials will result in less supplementation. In our recent three-state study of high school ELA teachers, Louisiana's teachers were far more likely to use high-quality materials than the average teacher in Massachusetts or Rhode Island, but they were only a bit less likely to modify their materials in most ways.[25] Still, the hope is that over time if teachers were receiving quality, well-aligned materials, supports for those materials, and opportunities to collaborate with colleagues around the implementation of those materials, that at least the ad hoc nature of teacher supplementation and modification might diminish somewhat.

THE CONSEQUENCES OF THESE BELIEFS AND PRACTICES

These two issues—teachers' historical curriculum control and their beliefs that all materials are flawed—may seem banal, but they have had important and pernicious consequences for the implementation of standards-based reform. That is, even if we could get a quality textbook in every teacher's hands, we would likely not see a quality enacted curriculum in every teacher's classes, at least given current prevailing attitudes. First, there is widespread and powerful resistance to the idea that any packaged curriculum should be used more or less with fidelity. Regardless of how good the materials are or how aligned to standards they are, there is agreement that no material should be used "as is" in the classroom—to the large majority of current teachers, doing so is tantamount to professional malpractice. This belief is undergirded by teachers' assertion of control over classroom instruction, and it is also undergirded by teachers' beliefs that their students are unique and require ongoing and extensive differentiation.

Once teachers accept that no full curriculum is good enough, the logical next conclusion is that they must either create one or find something better. And indeed, the evidence on supplementation makes it clear that essentially all teachers do so. But are supplemental materials any better than "prepackaged" ones? The truth is that we have basically no idea. There are very few studies at any kind of scale of the quality of supplemental materials, and there are none that I am aware of that focus on the materials individual teachers create themselves. I recently led a study where expert reviewers analyzed the content and quality of the most-used high school ELA materials on three popular supplemental materials websites, and that study found that just under two-thirds of the materials were not worth using.[26] Materials fell short in their coverage of standards, in their supports for teacher implementation, and in their appropriateness for diverse learners. Were these materials better or worse than the materials teachers were using them to replace? The answer depends on many things, not the least of which is how the materials were used. But by and large, it is not knowable and never can be known at anything approaching scale. Still, it's very clear that these materials fell short in a number of ways. And it seems highly unlikely that less-popular materials or materials from less-used websites would be any better.

There are several reasons to think that this issue is almost fatally damaging to the goal of standards implementation. The first reason is almost tautological, but nonetheless important—if a goal of standards is consistency across classrooms, consistency cannot be furthered by millions of teachers choosing or creating curricula individually. It is certainly possible that teaching and learning could be better, on average, in a world where standards implementation was worse. But it is inconceivable that standards implementation is made better when teachers exercise greater discretion in selecting and implementing curriculum.

The second reason is that this clearly requires substantial effort and expense on the part of teachers. The process of identifying the weaknesses of curriculum materials and then seeking, selecting, and modifying supplemental materials is onerous, and teachers make clear that they wish they didn't have to do it so often (hence the data from our teacher interviews that teachers overwhelmingly wanted access to a quality core curriculum).[27] It's also costly—teachers spend billions of dollars of their own money on these materials (a bit less than $500 a year in total, though not all of this is on lessons or instructional materials).[28] Teachers would have more time to understand, collaborate, and modify their core instructional materials if they did not feel they had to spend so much time selecting other materials to implement. And they would have more money in their pockets, too.

The third reason is that this kind of approach to curriculum implementation—one heavily reliant on supplementation to meet student needs—almost undoubtedly exacerbates other well-known policy problems. For instance, teacher observation and evaluation are almost entirely neutered by the lack of a common curriculum. Because we cannot rely on teachers to be teaching similar content, our instructional protocols must rely on general, high-level practices that are divorced from what teachers are supposed to be teaching. In other words, it would be one thing to evaluate pedagogical quality in a context in which teachers are roughly teaching the same things; it's another thing entirely to evaluate quality when it's confounded by the materials the teacher has chosen. And it's also more difficult to support teachers to improve their instruction (in preservice, in-service, or coaching interactions) when everyone is implementing different things. It forces these kinds of supports to be generic in their content focus in ways that likely undermine their helpfulness. The high degree of supplementation also likely contributes to the stratification of student opportunity to learn—research shows that teachers of more disadvantaged students supplement more often, and they report doing so more frequently because they believe the adopted materials are too challenging for their students.[29]

In short, our attitude toward curriculum—what we want it to look like, how we expect teachers to interact with it, what we believe about its relationship to standards implementation—is seriously flawed. There cannot be strong and coherent implementation of any instructional target, let alone one as complex as a set of content standards, across tens of thousands of schools and millions of teachers, without high-quality materials at the center. Without a curriculum-oriented approach to standards implementation, teachers' work is made all but impossible and students' opportunity to learn suffers.

CHAPTER 5

The Lack of Support for Coherence

Implementing standards is hard work, for all of the reasons we've already discussed. For teachers to be able to do it right, they need support. They need support to understand the standards, to sequence them, to decide how much emphasis to place on individual standards and strands. They need support to implement their chosen curriculum materials, and, given the universal prevalence of supplementation and modification, to find ways to differentiate their implementation for students with different needs and to supplement their curriculum thoughtfully.

Teachers don't get any of this support, at least not the levels and quality of support they need to implement the standards as intended. And key features of the system get in the way of ever providing it, so there is little reason to think that technical fixes to the ways we support teachers will lead to much better outcomes. This chapter is all about the support teachers need that they're not getting. In describing what's missing, the chapter also foreshadows my recommendations for how teachers can be better supported moving forward.

UNDERSTANDING THE STANDARDS

Teachers are the frontline implementers of standards in the classroom. Teachers' daily decisions—both planning and in the moment—determine what content students get exposed to, and whether that content is aligned with standards. Of course, teachers' decisions about what content to teach are influenced by a whole host of things—state and district policies, teachers' own prior experiences and beliefs, and their understanding of what the standards are asking them to do. In loosely coupled systems like the ones we have to guide teachers' instruction, where there is very little direct control of teachers' instructional decisions, teacher understanding—and the ability of teachers to translate that understanding into practice—is essential.

Unfortunately, research makes very clear that teachers (and, indeed, other actors in our schools and districts) don't always understand what the standards are asking them to do. This is not necessarily their fault—the standards are hard to understand, and our systems have inadequately supported teachers to understand them (setting aside that it's not at all obvious that it makes sense to rely on millions of individuals developing individualized and deep knowledge of the standards to have any hope of effective implementation).

Here are two pieces of evidence that teachers have not been supported to develop the important understanding of state standards that would be necessary for them to be able to implement them with fidelity. First, researchers at RAND lead periodic nationally representative survey studies through the American Teacher Panel.[1] This is a well-run study that reflects the population of US K–12 public school teachers. On their 2016 and 2017 surveys, researchers asked the panel of teachers a series of questions meant to gauge their knowledge of the standards they were supposed to be teaching. In mathematics, they asked teachers to consider four standards and indicate which of the four standards was aligned with the grade level they taught. The trick was that two of the four standards were straight out of their grade-level standards, while the other two ("distractors") were drawn from one or two grade levels above or below. For instance, eighth-grade teachers were shown four standards: "represent and analyze quantitative relationships between dependent and independent variables" (a grade 6 standard);

"define, evaluate, and compare functions" (grade 8); "understand and apply the Pythagorean theorem" (grade 8); and "understand that a set of data collected to answer a statistical question has a distribution, which can be described by its center, spread, and overall shape" (grade 6). Teachers were marked as "correct" if they identified both of their grade-level standards and none of the distractors.

The results were sobering. Of the eighth-grade mathematics teachers in the sample, just 1 percent got the correct answer. The results in other grades were better, but overall across the almost five hundred mathematics teachers surveyed, only 41 percent correctly responded to this question.[2] There was a slight improvement from 2016 to 2017 (from 36 percent to 41 percent), but at that pace of growth it would take until 2029—until an entire cohort of students had passed from kindergarten through to high school graduation—for the content aims of the standards to have been fully internalized by those tasked with implementing them. Given that the standards were adopted in most states no later than 2012, and Common Core State Standards tests were implemented everywhere by 2015, states clearly have not done what they need to in order to get teachers to understand these key goals at scale.

Second, as mentioned earlier, I recently led an interview study of California eighth-grade math teachers. The interviews had multiple goals, but one key goal was to understand what teachers thought the Common Core math standards were asking them to do and how they were modifying their instruction to respond to the standards. Specifically, we asked them, "How do you see the new standards influencing the way you plan and deliver your lessons? What do you view as the major instructional changes called for by the standards, as compared to California's prior content standards?" If we didn't get specific content-related answers, we typically probed teachers with, "What are the differences between the new standards and previous standards?"

Again, the results did not give us much confidence that the districts in our sample had equipped teachers with a deep understanding of the standards. By far the most common answer to our questions was that the Common Core required more student-directed learning than prior standards. It is debatable whether this is true, but certainly the standards themselves are agnostic on who is supposed to be directing classroom instruction, indeed claiming the standards "do not dictate how teachers should teach. Instead, schools and teachers will decide how best to help students reach the standards."[3] The second most common answer was that under Common Core students now had to explain their work or communicate their rationale. It is true that Common Core includes "math practices" such as "construct viable arguments." In short, teachers heavily emphasized the process differences between new and old standards.

When we probed teachers for specific content differences between old standards and new standards, most teachers said there were none (e.g., "algebra is algebra"), had no answer, or continued to talk about process differences. It was infrequent that we heard specific and correct answers about content shifts between the new and the old standards. In fact, just 31 percent of teachers offered a response that accurately described a content difference between new and old standards. This was especially remarkable given that the study took place in California, where the prior state standards did not even include grade-specific eighth-grade standards (instead, all of the standards for grades 8–12 were presented together by subdomain). Many teachers responded that Common Core was what they were already doing, that it was "just good teaching."

Where did these beliefs about the math standards come from? We did not ask teachers this question directly, but there are a few reasonable hypotheses based on other data. First, district leaders in these teachers' districts rarely elaborated specific standards-aligned professional learning opportunities they'd offered, and indeed most teachers in the United States don't receive much standards-, curriculum-, or content-focused training (more on this below). So teachers may simply not have been given the support to understand the new shifts in the standards, or they may have been given faulty support. Second, teachers in general tend to incorporate new practices alongside old ones, so it may be that they responded that Common Core math is "just good teaching" because they think of themselves as good teachers and do not want to question whether the standards require more fundamental instructional changes. And third, following on the last chapter, actually sitting down and reading and comparing sets of standards to identify content differences is not the easiest task, and teachers probably have not done much of it.

These two studies are not the only ones that indicate fundamental problems with educators' understanding of standards. Studies going back to the NCLB era and before have highlighted the difficulty in interpreting state standards. For instance, Heather C. Hill documented the ways that committees of educators puzzled over the meaning of specific words and objectives in state standards and often adopted interpretations that seemed at odds with what the writers of the standards likely intended.[4] As an example, verbs like "construct, develop, explain," which were often included by standards authors to encourage or imply a more student-constructed approach to teaching and learning, were often interpreted in ways that did not challenge the teacher-directed instruction that seemed to predominate. James P. Spillane found that teachers' understandings of standards policy were heavily influenced by districts' understandings and documented the ways that the multiple levels separating teachers from the policy often resulted in misunderstandings of the policy's intent.[5] These findings, then, are not new, but it is important to note that another two decades have elapsed since Hill's and Spillane's work and we are seeing the same problems.

THE COMPLEXITY OF STANDARDS

A majority of teachers, nearly a decade into the implementation of new standards, do not know what the standards are asking them to do. The rest of this chapter explains the many reasons why this is so. Again, some of these points have been covered before in earlier standards eras, but it is worth emphasizing that the problems still exist to perhaps just as strong a degree even though we have been trying as a nation to implement standards since East and West Germany were still separate nations.[6]

The first, and most obvious, reason is that standards are simply complicated and difficult to understand. There are a number of ways in which they are complicated. One is that individual objectives are often not very clear. For instance, while likely any eighth-grade mathematics teacher understands "apply the Pythagorean theorem to find the distance between two points in a coordinate system," many probably struggle with this standard:

Understand that patterns of association can also be seen in bivariate categorical data by displaying frequencies and relative frequencies in a two-way table. Construct and interpret a two-way table summarizing data on two categorical variables collected from the same subjects. Use relative frequencies calculated for rows or columns to describe possible association between the two variables.

How many objectives are straightforward and how many objectives are tricky is in the eye of the beholder, but I encourage the reader to go read a set of content standards and see what they think about the objectives. Many of them require some interpretation or at least careful thought before they can be understood, and the multiple layers of governance separating the text of the standards from the readers and implementers of the standards (i.e., teachers) undoubtedly increase the extent to which there can be misinterpretations.

Another way that standards are complicated is that they often have at least one other dimension in addition to the objectives, and it is not clear how teachers should treat multidimensional standards. For instance, in mathematics, the Common Core standards also have "standards for mathematical practice" (SMPs) that are layered on top of the objectives. These SMPs, which are the same for each grade, describe "varieties of expertise that mathematics educators at all levels should seek to develop in their students."[7] (Non–Common Core states, like Texas and Virginia, have similar "process standards.") In ELA, there are guidelines about text complexity and around the allocation of emphasis across literature versus informational text. In science, the Next Generation Science Standards proudly emphasize their three-dimensional structure, which includes crosscutting concepts (e.g., "cause and effect"), science and engineering practices (i.e., what scientists and engineers do), and disciplinary core ideas (what you might think of as most parallel to the mathematics objectives mentioned above). These two- or three-dimensional structures may be important, but they certainly muddy the water in terms of teachers' ability to understand what the standards are asking them to do.

Third, standards documents generally do not offer guidance on relative emphasis, nor on organization. Again, considering the eighth-grade

Common Core math standards, there are thirty-three objectives (or thirty-six depending on how you count). These range in breadth from the very narrow ("Know and apply the properties of integer exponents to generate equivalent numerical expressions. For example, $3^2 \times 3^{-5} = 3^{-3} = 1/3^3 = 1/27$.") to the very broad ("Construct a function to model a linear relationship between two quantities. Determine the rate of change and initial value of the function from a description of a relationship or from two (x, y) values, including reading these from a table or from a graph. Interpret the rate of change and initial value of a linear function in terms of the situation it models, and in terms of its graph or a table of values."). While it is obvious from just looking at these objectives that one should spend more time covering the latter than the former, there is no guidance in the document itself. So teachers' implementation of these objectives will depend on teachers' views on the relative importance of the two pieces of content, among other things.

Similarly, there is nothing in standards documents generally about how teachers should organize these thirty-three objectives in a year's instruction. Presumably there are better and worse ways to organize these objectives, but there is no indication of that in the document itself. Thus, the coherence with which the objectives are organized and delivered to students will be a result of teachers' choices about sequencing (which may be good or bad).

It is worth pausing for a moment to think about why standards have been written in this way that is plainly too complicated for teachers to use easily. I think the simplest explanation is that standards currently have to speak to too many audiences. They have to represent the ways that subject matter experts—mathematicians, scientists, scholars of reading and writing—think about and organize the subject. They have to be small enough in number that teachers can look at them and think they can get through them in a school year (indeed, "fewer" was one of the stated goals of the Common Core). They can't be so specific that they are seen as limiting teachers' autonomy, so they have to have a certain degree of vagueness. But regardless of the reason, in being so complex and in offering such little guidance, the standards doom themselves to poor implementation and irrelevance.

In short, in order for standards to be implemented well, the current approach to standards implementation requires that individual teachers make sense of the standards. But this is obviously, and on its face, not a way to get anything approaching standardization. The standards simply do not contain enough detail and guidance for there to be standardized inter- pretation, and this is a primary reason why teachers do not have common (or often, correct) understandings of what the standards are asking them do. If standards writers wanted teachers to have a common understanding, the least they could have done would have been to create detailed, specific guidance for how the standards should be interpreted and implemented. But to have done so would have raised the twin specters of the "scripted curriculum" and the "national curriculum," and thus it was not done.

THE LACK OF SUPPORT FOR TEACHERS TO UNDERSTAND AND IMPLEMENT THE STANDARDS

There are a number of supports that teachers could be receiving to imple- ment standards in ways that are more in line with what policy makers would like. They could be given high-quality, standards-aligned curricu- lum materials. They could receive necessary aligned supports within those materials, like assessments and teachers' guides. They could receive stan- dards-aligned preservice teacher education and in-service professional learning opportunities. They could be given feedback on how to better sup- port diverse student groups to master the standards. Their teacher evalu- ations could align with the standards. Their schools' or districts' interim or benchmark assessments could align with the standards. They could be in schools that simply have the enabling conditions—a collegial environ- ment, time for collaboration, leadership focused on learning—that facili- tate aligned instruction.[8]

Unfortunately, research suggests that the average school setting falls short on many, most, or all of these elements of coherence. Using data from the 2019 American Teacher Panel in three states (Louisiana, Massachusetts, and Rhode Island), I recently led a team to investigate this very issue, ask- ing to what extent teachers experience coherent instructional systems that support standards implementation.[9] In our case, we were focused on ELA instruction. We investigated the coherence of teachers' instructional sys- tems by looking at multiple indicators:

- Whether they had access to and used curriculum materials that were rated as "standards aligned" by expert reviewers
- Whether they thought their curriculum materials—whatever they were—were aligned with state standards and assessments
- How much and what kind of professional learning they received, and to what extent they thought it was helpful
- To what extent their school demonstrated the presence of factors thought to enable instructional coherence

We asked how teachers varied along these different dimensions and also whether teachers' answers varied by state, grade level, and the kinds of students they served. We also asked district leaders in each state similar questions. In total, our results reflected survey responses from 774 teachers and 140 district leaders across the three states.

Our results demonstrated remarkably low levels of most of these dimensions of instructional coherence and support. Starting with the core curriculum materials, just over one-third of district leaders (39 percent) reported requiring or recommending at least one material that EdReports.org had rated as standards aligned. The proportion was much higher in Louisiana (80 percent of district leaders) than in Massachusetts (19 percent) or Rhode Island (25 percent). These numbers were similarly reflected in teachers' responses. Just 34 percent of teachers overall said they regularly used at least one standards-aligned material, and far more in Louisiana than in the other two states. The lack of provision of standards-aligned materials left teachers responsible for creating their own. In Massachusetts and Rhode Island, in fact, teachers were more likely to say they used self-created materials than they were to use materials EdReports had rated as standards-aligned.[10] In the higher grades teachers were especially unlikely to use standards-aligned core materials and especially likely to use teacher-created materials. About half of Louisiana and Rhode Island high school teachers and about three-quarters of Massachusetts high school teachers reported using teacher-created materials.

Not surprisingly given these numbers, teachers were only modestly in agreement that their main instructional materials were well aligned with state standards or assessments. Less than one-third of teachers strongly agreed that their main instructional materials helped students master the standards or covered the content in state summative assessments (with about half of teachers only "somewhat" agreeing). Though, given the results reported above, teachers' ratings of the alignment of materials should be taken with a large grain of salt, these findings at least clearly indicate that teachers do not feel they have the curricular support needed to teach an aligned curriculum.

Neither did teachers receive the kind of professional development on their core curriculum materials that would help them implement the materials more effectively. We have long known that multiday professional development is more likely to result in growth in teacher knowledge and practice than professional development that is shorter in duration.[11] And yet 57 percent of teachers in our survey reported that they had not had professional learning over multiple days on their curriculum materials (and just 6 percent reported that they had received this kind of professional development more than a few times). And when they did receive professional development of this sort, half of teachers said it was only slightly effective or not effective at all. Teachers were much more likely to report that they received common planning time (about a third of teachers reported they received this weekly) or professional learning communities (about a sixth of teachers got this weekly) than any kind of specific training or support on their curriculum materials. While these may be useful instructional supports for teachers, they were still far from prevalent for the average teacher across the three states.

We also asked teachers about three other kinds of instructional supports that would facilitate their implementation of their core instructional materials. The first was curriculum-related support they might receive either through their core instructional materials or from their schools or districts: lesson plans, online software, pacing guides, assessments, suggested remediation activities (based on assessment results or not), and help anticipating student responses. While all teachers reported receiving some of these curriculum-related supports, several were less common. For instance, just 52 percent of teachers reported receiving lesson plans, and just 51 percent reported receiving help anticipating student responses. (In other words, about half of teachers may receive core materials, but they do not receive detailed lesson plans that would help them implement those materials in their classrooms). In general, whether teachers received these resources seemed to be more about what book they were using than what district they were located in—some materials simply come with more kinds of supports than others. The second support we asked about was the alignment of their interim or benchmark assessments with state standards and assessments. Only half of teachers—50 percent—said their interim assessments aligned to a large extent with the content of state ELA standards. The numbers were worse for state tests, where just 42 percent of teachers said they aligned to a large extent. And the third support was teacher evaluation. While most teachers (77 percent) said their evaluations focused to at least a moderate extent on "the alignment of their instruction to state standards," only about half (56 percent) said the same for "how much they follow school system curriculum guidance."

In order to have any hope of instructional coherence, teachers must be in schools and districts that have the kinds of supporting policies and cultures that research shows are essential for success. We asked about these "enabling factors" as well, and the results, shown below in table 5.1, were even more troubling. Of the seven factors we asked about, the most common was "goals for student learning that are clear for everyone." Still, just 25 percent of respondents said that was present to a large extent in their schools. For several factors, a majority of teachers indicated they were present either not at all or to a slight extent: "leaders who model learning" (64 percent), "structures and processes that support educator collaboration" (56 percent), and "a set of teaching practices that are used by all" (55 percent). Across all the items on the scale, the average response was smack in the middle, halfway between "present to a slight extent" and "present to a moderate extent." And in fact less than a third of all teachers—just 31 percent—responded "present to a moderate extent" or higher on average across the seven items. To be sure, some of these are ambitious factors that are not easy to cultivate, but the fact is that very few teachers are in school settings that provide them with the conditions to even begin to work toward coherent instruction.

TABLE 5.1. Percentage of ELA teachers in Louisiana, Massachusetts, and Rhode Island reporting the presence of enabling factors for coherence.

	Not present	Present to a slight extent	Present to a moderate extent	Present to a large extent
A shared purpose that drives action	15	29	37	19
A small number of goals that are tied to ELA student learning	13	31	39	17
Leaders who model learning	33	31	26	10
Structures and processes that support educator collaboration	17	39	31	13
Goals for student learning that are clear for everyone	11	27	37	25
A set of teaching practices that are used by all	20	35	30	15
Processes such as examination of student work are used to improve practice	17	32	32	19

Source: American Teacher Panel survey of Louisiana, Massachusetts, and Rhode Island teachers. *Note: n* = 774 teachers. Survey item: "To what extent are the following present in your school to support your ELA instruction?"

To illustrate just how dire the situation is with respect to the level of support schools and districts provide teachers to implement standards and curriculum well, we used the results from the questions above to group teachers into eight different profiles using the following three 1/0 indicators:

- Whether a teacher reported regularly using a standards-aligned curriculum
- Whether a teacher reported at least two of the following four policy supports: receiving at least four of seven possible curriculum-related supports, receiving at least one multiday curriculum-related professional development activity, having interim assessments at least moderately aligned with other instructional supports, and having

evaluations focused on instructional alignment and supporting diverse students to at least a moderate extent

- Whether a teacher reported that the seven enabling conditions for coherence listed in table 5.1 were present to at least a moderate extent

These data could then be analyzed by giving teachers a total score from 0 to 3 or by examining the distribution of teachers across the eight profiles represented by the three indicators. From this analysis, we reached several conclusions.

First, very few teachers had a score of 3—just 14 percent of the respondents. To the naive eye, the indicators do not look like they represent a very high bar—use an aligned curriculum, be in a policy environment that moderately supports your implementation of that curriculum, and be in a school that has a moderate degree of enabling conditions. And yet only one in seven teachers in our sample could meet that bar. Another 31 percent of teachers had a score of 2; 34 percent had a score of 1; and 21 percent had a score of 0. In short, teachers were 50 percent more likely to have none of these three indicators of instructional coherence than they were to have all of them, and the majority of teachers had either zero or one indicator.

Second, looking at the marginal probabilities for the three categories, it was clear that teachers' settings especially fell short on having aligned materials and on having the enabling conditions for instructional coherence. Just 36 percent of teachers regularly used a standards-aligned curriculum, and just 31 percent had the enabling conditions to at least a moderate extent. In contrast, 72 percent of teachers had two of the four policy supports (though two of four supports is hardly an overwhelming degree of policy coherence).[12]

And third, we saw very large differences across states (and to a lesser extent grade levels and classroom characteristics) in terms of teachers' access to these three indicators of coherence. State policy was a major driver, with Louisiana teachers substantially more likely to have all three indicators (33 percent) than Massachusetts (1 percent) or Rhode Island (7 percent) teachers. Louisiana teachers were also more likely to have two or more indicators (74 percent versus 27 percent in Massachusetts and 28 percent in Rhode Island) and less likely to have zero indicators (4 percent versus 32 percent in Massachusetts and 26 percent in Rhode Island). This aligns with other research highlighting Louisiana's policy efforts to drive instructional coherence.[13] Elementary school teachers also seemed to have higher levels of coherence in their instructional systems than middle and high school teachers (largely because they were more likely to receive curriculum-related supports), and teachers of more students with disabilities had lower levels of coherence in their systems than teachers of fewer students with disabilities.

In short, our takeaway from this research was that vanishingly few teachers have access to a policy system that supports instructional coherence. They lack standards-aligned materials and they lack school settings that give them the conditions needed to practice aligned instruction. As discussed above, they also lack key knowledge about the standards and what the standards are asking them to do. Given that we have been doing standards for decades, the continued absence of these factors should be a shocking wake-up call and raise the question—if we cannot achieve this low bar of support by now, can we ever?

THE PARTICULAR CASE OF PROFESSIONAL DEVELOPMENT

Whenever there is a widely acknowledged issue with respect to teachers, the somewhat flippant solution is always professional development. And indeed, it's true that teachers need ongoing professional development in order to improve their practice. Teachers don't receive much professional learning on their curriculum—as mentioned above, for our three-state study the majority of teachers reported zero multiday training activities related to their curriculum.[14] Another recent six-state study (this one in elementary mathematics) similarly found that teachers had received an average of 1.1 days of professional development on their curriculum materials in the last year (and just over three days over their entire careers, on average).[15] So, teachers probably are not getting enough professional development on their curriculum (let alone the standards).

But it is not just about quantity where teachers' professional learning supports are falling short. Research for several decades has pulled out key features of effective professional development activities.[16] One is the content focus of the professional development—research suggests professional development is more effective to the extent that it focuses on subject matter content, how students learn that content, and how to effectively teach that content. A second is the extent to which the learning experiences are active (e.g., including observation, discussion, or practicing what was learned) versus passive (i.e., lecture-oriented), with the former demonstrating more effectiveness. A third is the coherence of the learning experiences with other initiatives and policies in the school or district. And a fourth is the degree to which teachers participate collectively in the professional learning, with more collective participation leading to greater implementation and effects. Along most of these dimensions, teachers describe professional learning experiences in practice that do not align with what research suggests would be most effective.

Another of the topics in our interview study of California teachers was about the professional development they'd received, both about the standards themselves and about their curriculum materials.[17] In terms of prevalence, we reached similar conclusions to the survey studies—most teachers received at least some curriculum-related professional development (in our study it was just over 60 percent of teachers representing 80 percent of participating districts who reported receiving any). Far fewer teachers—just about one in five—reported receiving professional development specifically relating to state standards. This evidence supports the survey findings in suggesting that teachers are not getting the quantity of professional development that they likely need to meaningfully improve their instruction.

But teachers' responses to our interview questions shed some additional light on why the professional development they were receiving, both about the curriculum and about the standards, was less helpful than it could have been. Some common examples of ineffective professional development included:

- Professional development that focused mainly on superficial characteristics of the textbook, like how it was organized or formatted, or the many new bells and whistles that came with the book
- Professional development that seemed canned or otherwise not related to the realities of implementing the materials in a classroom or in the specific school or district context

- Professional development delivered by trainers without sufficient experience or content expertise to be trustworthy

Teachers were especially critical of professional development that was passive in nature—where they received a lecture or demonstration of materials without the opportunity to try it out and discuss it with colleagues.

The teachers in our sample, whether implicitly or explicitly, seemed aware of what the literature had to say about effective professional development, but it was not what they were getting. They were not getting professional development that was focused on how to effectively teach the standards or the curriculum—they were mostly getting superficial instruction that they felt they didn't need. They were not getting professional development that was extensive in duration—they were mostly getting training over no more than a couple days at one point in time. They were not getting professional development that involved them practicing the curriculum, discussing it with colleagues, or observing quality instruction—they were mostly getting lectures or demonstrations that they felt were unhelpful.

To be sure, a few teachers described professional development related to curriculum materials that they found to be effective. Most often this effective professional development involved multiple days, focused on curriculum implementation, included problem-solving activities based on teacher experiences, and involved collaboration with other teachers using the same materials. One teacher described it this way:

> You attend the follow-up session and then they will ask you what happened, where are you now. Then we share what works, what didn't work, what's your suggestion, which topics you want to skip—things like that. It's like collaboration with teachers from other schools. You know that you're not alone having those problems.

This kind of rich professional learning experience was often associated with particular curricula (in this case it was College Preparatory Mathematics) that were seen as requiring especially profound shifts in instruction. It has the hallmarks of effective professional development—extensive duration (and continuously throughout the year), collective participation, focus on content and instruction, and active learning. This learning experience, while seemingly optimal, was very rare—teachers in just two of the more than thirty districts described curriculum-oriented professional learning experiences that aligned this strongly with the characteristics of effective professional development.

WHY DON'T WE SUPPORT TEACHERS HOW THEY NEED TO BE SUPPORTED?

There is no question that teachers need robust professional learning experiences to implement curriculum or standards well. That is, by and large, not what they have been getting. There are many reasons for this failure, but none of those reasons are because we don't know what works. The research on professional development has known these core characteristics for two decades. And, more to the point, teachers know it themselves, and they'll gladly tell you what works for them if you ask them about it. The reasons for the failure of professional development to effectively serve as a support for teachers are multiple, but here I highlight just a few.

One reason that professional development often is delivered in forms that do not provide what teachers actually need (or that we know work to drive better instruction) is that leaders at all levels of the education system often take a more technical—as opposed to adaptive—approach to the implementation of instruction policies.[18] By technical approaches, I mean approaches that treat the problem as one that can be solved through the application of existing solutions, procedures, tools, and expert guidance. This stands in contrast to adaptive approaches, which require leaders and stakeholders to collaboratively experiment with new procedures, norms, or beliefs to address problems of practice with unknown solutions. In other words, if the solution to poorly aligned instruction is to simply adopt a curriculum and a publisher-offered professional development program and think that will result in the desired instructional outcomes, that is a technical approach. If the solution instead is to carefully consider the interconnected issues that contribute to the problem—weak curriculum and professional development but also teacher beliefs about students and curriculum, bell schedules, and the like—and construct solutions that are evolving and ongoing, that is a more adaptive approach.

In recent work, my colleagues and I conducted case studies of five districts spread across the country focused on their curriculum and standards implementation.[19] We found that it was much more common for districts to take technical approaches to curriculum and standards implementation, and that these technical strategies often undermined serious instructional improvement. For instance, districts taking a technical approach might mandate strict implementation of the adopted curriculum and hold teachers accountable if they are not implementing it well. This results in the curriculum being implemented, but it gets in the way of teachers flexibly modifying the curriculum as needed for their particular students. It also creates fear and confusion among teachers, so when strategies change—when the district eases off the pressure or adopts a new curriculum—there is confusion about what teachers should do. A different approach that we saw was to expect strict fidelity in year one of a new curriculum but with the clear expectation that teachers would be able to (and encouraged to) modify it in years two and beyond. Teachers in this latter district were also specifically supported by district-provided instructional coaches to ensure a degree of coherence across schools and grades.

Professional learning can similarly be treated as technical or adaptive, and it takes the former focus more often than the latter. Technical approaches to professional development are exemplified by the publisher-provided training focusing on superficial features like how to use the online platform. Districts know they need to provide some professional learning when they choose a new curriculum, so they go with the lowest-hanging fruit, which is whatever the publisher is offering. Adaptive approaches, in contrast, focus on collaboration around problems of instructional practice and embody the kinds of professional development supports we know work well. These approaches might involve teams of district leaders working together to make sense of the curriculum and deliver locally tailored supports that are more likely to drive teacher buy-in. In short, professional development is often of limited utility because leaders often pursue technically oriented professional development rather than considering the ways that professional learning can be a part of an adaptive leadership strategy.

Another reason that professional learning often falls short in terms of effectiveness is simply because it takes place in the decentralized structures that define our education system. Districts are often left on their own to plan and execute professional learning, but many districts are small and do not have the capacity to create or deliver it internally. Instead they often rely on outside providers who are, almost by definition, providing lowest-common-denominator training that is not deep or sustained. Higher levels of the system (e.g., counties or states) are not well positioned to provide this support to districts because the dozens or hundreds of districts under their purview may well use dozens of different curricula. They can offer standards-oriented professional development, but it will necessarily be disconnected from the curricula that most districts are using. Unless many districts are using a given curricula or taking a given approach to implementing the standards, there is no one at a higher level to provide the kinds of guidance and support that could reduce demands on districts to do it themselves and result in better-quality and more coherent support than can be provided by thirteen thousand districts working independently.

In short, we have known for ages what good professional development looks like, and yet states and districts by and large do not provide it. Neither do teachers broadly teach in schools and districts that give them the supports needed for coherence. There is nothing that should make us think that these facts will change, and certainly not at the scale needed. And without them, there is no reason to believe we will see the kind of standards implementation the policy demands.

CHAPTER 6

A Grand Bargain for America's Teachers

The last three chapters have discussed some of the central—but less emphasized—reasons why standards are not being implemented in American schools. As discussed in chapter 3, standards are not being implemented because the standards movement did not meaningfully address the decentralization that is the defining characteristic of American education. Fifty states largely abdicated their authority over the actual teaching and learning taking place in the schools they run, refusing to even collect data to ensure that—at a high level—schools and districts are using materials that are passably aligned with standards. In response to this lack of state guidance, thousands of school districts built elaborate textbook adoption processes that are duplicative in effort and more often than not result in the adoption of materials that experts say aren't even aligned to standards. Thus, decentralized structures block quality materials from making their way to teachers' hands, send teachers conflicting messages about what to do, and thwart effective standards implementation.

As discussed in chapter 4, standards are not being implemented because teachers view all materials as flawed to some extent (how much of this view is because the materials actually are flawed is not clear). They see curriculum control as central to their professional identities and view supplementing, modifying, or constructing their own curriculum as an essential part of their jobs. The decentralized model from the state and district filters down to the classroom, with teachers placed in school structures that offer them precious little time for collaboration with colleagues around curriculum and instruction. Thus, we get the teacher spending hours a week searching Teachers Pay Teachers for materials of totally unknown quality that may or may not cohere with the core curriculum or with what other teachers in the building are doing. Core materials are just one source among many that can guide teachers' instruction, undermining anything approaching the consistency that the standards movement calls for.

And as discussed in chapter 5, standards are not being implemented because, thirty years into the standards movement, schools and districts are still providing inadequate and overly technical supports to teachers to understand and implement the standards. Because the standards are themselves vaguely written and offer close to zero guidance for how they should actually be understood and implemented, teachers often don't fully understand what the standards are asking them to do. This dovetails with chapter 4—teachers are strangely expected to become alignment experts without support on the one hand, while on the other hand the theory of standards implementation crumbles under the weight of millions of teachers developing their own understandings of what the standards are asking them to do. The totally foreseeable result is that teachers do not implement the standards or materials as intended—we have asked them to do the impossible, so they cannot do it. These facts have been true for the entire history of the standards movement, and they will not change anytime soon. More importantly, there is no reason to believe that our decentralized systems are even constructed in such a way as to allow change.

The remaining three chapters of the book discuss what we can do to make things right. If our goal really is a quality curriculum for every child, what tools and strategies can we pursue? What we are doing is not working and cannot work. What might?

MAKING TEACHING DOABLE

America's teachers are overworked. Data from the Organisation for Economic Co-operation and Development (OECD) show that American teachers rank fifth among thirty-six countries in the number of hours worked.[1] Elementary teachers in the United States are required to teach an average of about 1,000 hours a year, about 30 percent more than the international average. The gap is even larger for high school teachers—the US average of 966 hours is 45 percent higher than the international average. Not only do teachers work more total hours, but they spend a higher proportion of those hours in the classroom than the international average (about 48 percent, versus an international average of about 43 percent), leaving a smaller fraction of their time for planning, preparation, and collaboration.

Despite the large amount of work American teachers do relative to their international counterparts, they are comparatively poorly compensated. Though international comparisons on pay are challenging, there are a variety of pieces of evidence on this. Among the twenty-four OECD countries where these breakdowns are available, the United States ranks fifth from the bottom in the proportion of total education spending that goes to teacher compensation.[2] In the United States, just 54 percent of education dollars go toward teacher compensation, lower than the international average of 63 percent. While teacher salaries in the United States are near the international average, when compared with the salaries of other college graduates in their own countries, US teachers rank second from the bottom among all nations. In short, US teachers spend much more time teaching than their international peers, and they receive low to medium rates of compensation (that are especially low when teacher salaries are compared with the salaries of other people who have similar levels of education).

As described in the previous chapters, our teachers are also not supported well to implement quality curriculum. While most countries have national standards and a handful of core curriculum materials that are tightly coupled to the standards, we have a hodgepodge of standards by state and subject (if any standards at all) and a curriculum materials market almost wholly untethered from the standards. Teachers say they want core materials to rely on, but many of our teachers do not receive any such materials, especially in non-core subjects but even in the main subjects that are the focus of standards-based policy efforts. Whether they do or do not receive core materials, teachers get little training on curriculum and standards. Finally, teachers spend countless hours and their own dollars to modify, add to, or differentiate the materials they are given, and teachers' curriculum supplementation receives close to zero attention from either district leaders or researchers.

The end result of these features of American education is that the enacted curriculum—what students are actually taught on a daily basis, and how they are taught it—is close to unknown. From the secretary of education to state education chiefs, from county offices of education even down to district super- intendents, no one has much of an idea of what is actually happening in class- rooms. Walk into two classrooms in a given school—even classes in the same grade and subject—and you are likely to see radically different approaches to curriculum and instruction. What evidence we do have about the enacted curriculum is that it is systematically worse for historically disadvantaged stu- dent groups.[3] Low-income students, students of color, and students tracked into lower-level courses systematically receive worse opportunities to learn than their peers, and the consequences for their learning are devastating.[4]

Standards were supposed to solve these problems, but as I have laid out so far they clearly have not. And they clearly will not unless we do some- thing radically different. This is what the rest of the book is about. If we really believe that teaching and learning is at the heart of what schools do (which it is!), if we really believe that student opportunities are stratified by the instructional opportunities they receive (which they are!), and if we really believe that states and the federal government have the responsibility to provide a high-quality education to all children (which they do!), what can we do to ensure these things actually happen? And how can we ensure that our reforms make teachers' jobs more doable and more sustainable than they have been?

CURRICULUM AT THE CORE

The heart of any reform that seeks to improve instruction at scale must be high-quality core curriculum materials. This chapter discusses a curricu- lum-driven reform strategy that individual districts can pursue to drive instructional improvement. Importantly, even though this approach should work in individual districts, it is not the sort of approach that can work at a higher level, because of the decentralization issues discussed throughout. Addressing that problem is the focus of the next chapter.

High-quality core materials serve several important purposes that make them a better approach than standards to drive instructional change. First, and most obviously, instructional materials drive consistency much more effectively than standards do. While standards could in principle lead to teachers implementing consistent, coherent instruction, many other things have to go right in order for that to happen (and, as we have seen, those things have not happened in thirty years of trying to implement standards). In contrast, well-supported core curriculum materials make consistency and quality much likelier. For all the reasons discussed above, standards are too far removed from teachers' day-to-day instruction to drive consistency. They are too unclear. They are too nonspecific. They require too much teacher labor. Only documents that get much closer to teachers' day-to-day decision-making can possibly lead to the kind of consistency standards advocates say they want.

Second, high-quality core materials can reduce, or at minimum redirect, teachers' workload. Having a high-quality base to start from makes the work of delivering a quality instructional experience much easier and more efficient. This is most obvious in the case of beginning teachers, who often show up at the schoolhouse door in August only to find that they have nothing at the instructional core to guide their teaching. But even for the seasoned veteran, a standards-driven approach to instruction requires teachers to identify materials, sequence those materials, ferret out areas of misalignment, and fill in those alignment gaps. If instead there is a quality, thoughtfully sequenced set of materials given to each teacher, the task becomes one mainly of figuring out how those materials are and are not working well and differentiating that material for their specific students. It changes the curriculum approach from one of "building your own curriculum"—which is time- and labor-intensive and something we don't prepare teachers to do—to one of "implementing, learning, and implementing again"—an approach that can foster ongoing improvement in practice.

Third, high-quality core materials increase opportunities for coherence and collaboration that can drive instructional improvement. When teachers are all on the same page—not literally in lockstep, but given the same high-quality base to start from—they can more easily work with their colleagues in their schools, districts, or even states to implement and, as needed, modify those materials for their local contexts. We heard about this in our interviews of California teachers and school district leaders— adopting the same core materials throughout a district or in collaboration with neighboring districts gave them the opportunity to work together on implementation and to learn from each other's successes and failures. Adopting common materials can facilitate multiple kinds of coherence and collaboration. It can facilitate across-grade coherence and collaboration, because the materials across grades from a given curriculum are likely to be more aligned with one another than if teachers in different grades are drawing from different curriculum sources. And it can facilitate across-school coherence and collaboration, allowing teachers to work together within a district (which has the added benefit of helping mobile students). In addition, when two teachers are teaching from the same set of materials and achieve different results, there is a greater opportunity to learn from their different outcomes and implement the curriculum better the next time. There is also an opportunity to supplement together, or to learn from each other's supplementation efforts in the context of the core curriculum. In contrast, when teachers lack a core curriculum there are too many differences between their instruction and anyone else's to learn much of anything about what is working and why. Iterative instructional improvement through collaboration and comparison becomes more difficult.

Fourth, high-quality core materials offer the opportunity to more tightly and coherently couple instructional reforms with other policy reforms. For instance, core materials make it more feasible to deliver preservice and in-service teacher learning experiences that can more effectively support instruction. The Louisiana experience bears this out, where the state is offering curriculum-aligned professional development to all its teachers and, as a result, those teachers better understand the standards.[5] Again, preservice teachers may especially benefit from a curriculum-driven approach. Imagine if part of preservice elementary teacher education was learning about the two or three state-approved ELA and math curricula, how they work, and how they can be implemented. And then imagine those teachers arriving in a school that is actually using one of those curricula. Given that we know that teachers' preservice experiences are more impactful if they are aligned with their placements once they get to the classroom, such a tight coupling of preservice learning would almost certainly lead to better instruction and student outcomes.[6] Core curriculum materials can also facilitate alignment of assessment systems with instruction—assessing students on their progress against the core curriculum solves the common complaint that interim assessments are poorly aligned and do not match teachers' instructional content or pacing.[7]

Core Materials in Practice

I have studied standards implementation for over a decade, with a focus on measuring the alignment of teachers' instruction with standards and identifying the policies that can improve that alignment. A decade ago, curriculum was hardly a focus. The focus then was on other levers to improve instruction—mainly assessments, accountability, and teacher evaluation. As it has become clear that those reforms were falling short of driving instruction in desirable ways (and often doing just the opposite!), there has been a decided turn toward curriculum. In part this has been driven by a few high-quality research studies, all in elementary mathematics, which have mostly found that curriculum materials differ considerably in their effects on student achievement.[8] For instance, these studies have found effects in the range of .10 to .20 standard deviations—an effect approximately as large as the difference in effectiveness between a veteran and a novice teacher. These studies have also sometimes found that the effect of high-quality materials is stronger for more disadvantaged students—for instance, in a California study I participated in, the impact of the more effective textbook was about twice as large for students who were receiving free or reduced-price lunch as for those who were not.[9] Interestingly, the most recent and largest study did not find such effects, but the preponderance of the evidence suggests that textbooks do differ in their effects on student achievement.[10]

Over the last several years of my research, the benefits of a core curriculum beyond just student achievement gains became more readily apparent to me. The most powerful evidence came in a recent study that colleagues and I conducted of the implementation of college- and career ready standards across the United States.[11] One of the core parts of that broader project was a five-district case study, one district in each of five states, covering a range of different sizes and contexts. We spent four to five days in each district, observing classrooms and talking to teachers and school and district leaders.[12]

We set out to study what standards looked like in practice in these five diverse districts. What we observed made clear the importance of a core curriculum to establishing coherent, consistent, high-quality instruction in these schools. This is perhaps best exemplified by the case of one anonymous district from our study. This district served a seemingly unremarkable exurb of a large West Coast city. It's the kind of town that you'd drive right past on your way out of the city on the freeway. Mostly built in recent years, the town is full of subdivisions with stereotypical subdivision names like Oak Falls and River Crest. The downtown is perfectly quaint and clustered around an old train station, while the rest of the town is filled with the usual suburban big-box stores. Many of the subdivisions are coterminous with the elementary schools, so there is a real "neighborhood school" vibe to the place despite the houses tending to look somewhat cookie-cutter.

The school district is a rare elementary-only district with about a dozen schools serving around seven thousand students. It's one of four school districts in its immediate area, and it has a reputation for being the best of the four. Indeed, it's widely perceived as being one of the best in the state—it's won recent recognition from the state and from several organizations for its high performance, especially for students from disadvantaged groups.[13] In recent years it has scored at the top level on the state's school grading system, demonstrating high performance that seems to just keep going up.

Given its high performance and sterling reputation, you might expect the district to be highly affluent and lily-white—the sort of quasi-private district that keeps kids out by virtue of high property values. In fact, that's not the case at all. Almost half of the students (about 43 percent) receive free or reduced-price lunch. Neither is the district monochromatic—the student racial/ethnic diversity is high, with about 10 percent Asian students, 40 percent Hispanic students, and 10 percent other non-White races. About 30 percent of the district is English language learners (ELLs). The schools within the district vary considerably, however, from 95 percent low-income and 70 percent ELL at the most disadvantaged school to 10 percent low-income and 5 percent ELL at the most affluent.

What we saw in our week in the district was remarkable. High-quality, rigorous instruction in every general education classroom. Class-to-class consistency in terms of instructional approaches and content coverage. Engaged, well-behaved students at every grade level. Instructional supports for ELL students in every school, even in the most affluent school, where they constituted only a small proportion of the student body. Extra instructional supports in the schools serving the most disadvantaged students (most classrooms there had multiple adults in the room). The district seemed to be running like a well-oiled, tightly coupled machine focused on equitable opportunities and high-quality instruction.

What we heard, though, was even more remarkable. I've never been in a district where everyone spoke with such a consistent voice, such that by the fourth school visit we felt like we could answer the questions before we asked them. Teachers in the district were supported extensively, with ambitious and curriculum-oriented professional development. They received targeted coaching as needed (which turned out to be infrequently given the quality of the curriculum and the teachers) and across-the-board professional learning community time to go over student data and prepare instruction for the following week. In our interviews we routinely heard sentiments that endorsed the district's curriculum culture, which almost all agreed was focused on implementing the curriculum well, learning what worked and what didn't, and collaboratively identifying supplements to fill in the gaps:

> As far as the curriculum itself... we need to teach it with fidelity.... I like our curriculum, both ELA and math, and I make the changes where they need to be made.

> We all work together... It helps a lot... just having people who have done it for a year or two. Like even in our math curriculum, first year we did everything and then we said, no, we're not doing this one again. We're not doing this one. We need to supplement in this area. There's not enough coverage of this concept.

> Pretty much, we plan together... So it is planned that way that we all teach or pretty closely the same lesson in a day. So you could go into four third-grade classes and see... typically the same math lesson and the same objective.

To be sure, things were not perfect in the district. Students with disabilities were highly isolated, the district having just moved away from a long-standing policy of grouping students with similar disabilities together and shuffling them around from school to school each year (though they still scored well above the state average for this group). And there were some teachers (around 10–20 percent) who expressed concern about the district's reform policy or utilized the adopted curriculum with less fidelity than other teachers (though even in these classrooms, the instruction felt ambitious and high quality). But overall, this seemed to be a district doing impressive things to produce strong outcomes for all its students. It was a model to be emulated.

This district was one of two we observed that had core curriculum materials at the heart of their instructional reform efforts and adopted what we called a "flexibly specific" approach to implementing those materials. In these districts, teachers were supported with curriculum-aligned professional learning and coaching. This learning was ongoing, not just in the first year of implementation as it so often is, and it was delivered by internal experts rather than the dreaded publisher representatives. Furthermore, it evolved over time to focus on successes and challenges in implementing the materials as opposed to more superficial features. There was a clear strategy for how teachers were supposed to use the materials to drive standards implementation. In short, they were supposed to use the materials very faithfully in the first year of implementation and then to collaboratively supplement as needed in subsequent years. And that strategy was clearly communicated with teachers—not in a top-down way, but in a way that respected their professional authority and expertise and the knowledge they accumulated as they implemented the materials in their classrooms; I did not hear one teacher express resentment or distrust about the district's approach to curriculum.

The result of these efforts was that instruction was well organized and effectively delivered in every classroom we saw in these districts. Teachers were not in absolute lockstep, but they were in very close sequence with each other and regularly communicated about what was working and what was not. This was in part enabled by professional learning community time built into the school schedule, though teachers did emphasize that they wished they had more time for this purpose. They were not automata mindlessly implementing a script; they were professionals relying on their core materials for the foundation of their instruction and modifying as needed for their specific students. Though of course it is not possible to draw a direct line from these practices to student outcomes, these districts were recognized for their high performance on state report cards and by other organizations.[14]

The other districts we studied fell short of this ideal in various ways. In one district, though the central office had adopted particular materials, decisions about implementation came mostly from the school level. The result of this approach was that some schools relied on all-but-scripted curricula that teachers felt afraid not to implement with perfect fidelity, and other schools offered teachers no guidance at all on whether or how to use the adopted materials. In another district, curriculum just wasn't a focus, and you could tell from conversations with district leaders that they had little idea what was going on in their district's classrooms.

District-Led, Curriculum-Driven Reform

Based on this evidence, I believe there are several essential steps that school districts should take if they want to pursue a curriculum-driven approach to standards implementation. Importantly, these steps should be pursued across more subjects than just mathematics and ELA. Any subject important enough to teach is important enough to support with high-quality materials.

In terms of textbook adoption, one important suggestion is that there should be a clear and transparent process for adoption that involves teachers heavily. We found in our teacher interviews in California that teachers were more likely to support and use the adopted materials if they either played a role in adoption themselves or clearly understood the process and believed it was a quality process. This also showed up in our case-study districts, where there was strong trust in the adopted materials in part because teachers felt their voice was heard in the adoption decision. Another suggestion is that the process use evidence on textbook quality that has already been collected by others, including state department of education reviews or adoption lists, EdReports reviews, and feedback from other districts that have already made adoption decisions. There is very little reason to reanalyze materials for alignment when that work has already been done by folks trained to do it, and we saw little evidence that the Herculean review efforts districts often undertake result in better textbook adoption decisions being made. A third suggestion is that teachers be given the opportunity to pilot the candidate materials before adoption. This pilot need not be elaborate or overly long, but it must give teachers the opportunity to get the look and feel of the materials and identify the ways in which it works and doesn't work for their students.

In terms of curriculum implementation, the most important recommendation is that districts lay out clear expectations and plans for implementation and communicate them to teachers. One plan that seems to work well is to expect relatively faithful implementation of the adopted materials in the first year and then build in opportunities for modification and supplementation in subsequent years. Making sure that teachers are aware of these plans and understand the rationale behind them can ensure greater teacher support. Districts should support teachers with curriculum-oriented professional learning that follows the well-established principles of effective professional learning—it should be adequate in duration, involve teachers collectively, and utilize active learning methods.[15] Districts should also support teachers by building in the structures necessary to support collaboration—common planning time and professional learning communities, for instance. None of these suggestions is groundbreaking, but together they can have an impact on teachers' attitudes toward the adopted curriculum and their use of it.

THE THORNY PROBLEM OF SUPPLEMENTATION

If we want to put curriculum materials front and center in our reform efforts, we must pay attention to a few key issues. Here I focus specifically on issues affecting teachers' implementation of materials.

The main teacher-level issue that needs attention is teacher supplementation. Ideally, adopting better materials that are better supported would result in teachers feeling less compelled to supplement. There probably is some truth to that. Evidence clearly suggests that teachers' perceptions of the usability of textbooks, their alignment to standards, the difficulty of textbooks, and other factors affect the quantity and nature of teachers' supplementation.[16] But the truth is that supplementation is such a core part of US teachers' practices and identities that reducing supplementation will be a challenge. That said, there simply has to be greater effort to redirect teacher supplementation in ways that lead to better curriculum implementation. There are a number of potential strategies that could be pursued here.

One promising approach is for states to support better supplementation through the state textbook adoption process. When states first review materials for adoption decisions, they undoubtedly recognize areas of strength and weakness in each material. Rather than simply pointing these out, states can assemble committees of experts to either source or create supplemental materials to fill gaps in the adopted materials. These materials can be made freely available on state websites or through partnerships with outside organizations. Similarly, as materials are being implemented by teachers after state adoption, the state can set up procedures to take feedback from teachers about what is working, what is not, and what supplements seem to support better teaching (or this kind of work can be done through careful statewide pilots). For instance, a six-state study of textbook implementation found that significantly more teachers supplemented EngageNY in elementary mathematics because the textbook is too hard and because the textbook is not user-friendly relative to other common materials.[17] The state, seeing these issues, could develop or identify supplemental materials that include more scaffolds to support struggling students and that provide teachers with more of the kinds of user supports they need to implement the materials better. This approach would reduce the need for teachers to search for supplements by offering them directly. Over time, the more effective supplements could become integrated into the core materials themselves. For instance, a teacher could turn to a lesson and immediately be given multiple supplementation options corresponding to particular student needs in their classroom.

Districts can also be involved in supporting teachers to supplement in ways that reinforce, rather than undermine, the core curriculum. At a minimum, districts must give teachers the time and resources they need to supplement collaboratively, as mentioned above. This could mean working on a master schedule that ensures that teachers of a given grade and subject have time to work together to identify where supplementation is needed and to source supplemental materials. But district and school instructional leaders must also establish clear expectations for teachers about what forms of supplementation are encouraged and discouraged. For instance, a school might say that teachers should use supplemental materials only from a given set of websites that have adequate levels of overall quality. Though research on supplemental materials sites is far from promising about the quality of these materials, there is some evidence that the more regulated sites' materials are better in various ways than less regulated sites' materials.[18] School and district leaders might worry about micromanaging instruction in this way, but it is well within the authority of district curriculum leaders to ensure their teachers are using only high-quality materials in the classroom.

Another approach might come from the supply side—the materials producers themselves. Textbook publishers are struggling under the weight of the supplementation movement, coupled with online options and the perception that their early Common Core materials were insufficiently aligned to the standards. As yet, the response of the major publishers to the supplementation phenomenon seems to have been to throw their hands in the air and grant that their materials will be supplemented with other people's products. There is no reason that publishers cannot offer more differentiation and supports within their own materials to try to reduce the need for supplementation and keep teachers' attention and efforts within the covers of the textbook itself. As district leaders often acknowledge that the textbooks' supports for differentiation (especially for diverse populations like ELLs) were a major factor driving adoption decisions, offering more of these kinds of supports could also increase educators' interest in actually adopting and using publishers' materials.[19]

Regardless of these efforts, it would be naive to suggest that we can or should want to eliminate teachers' supplementation or modification activities. Rather, the goal is—or should be—to ensure that these activities improve, not diminish, the quality of the curriculum that is actually enacted for students. This does mean more oversight over supplementation than is currently offered (though there could hardly be less), but it does not mean prohibiting teachers' ability to flexibly implement the core materials. This will be a thorny issue for state, district, and school leaders to navigate.

CAUTIONS AND CONCERNS ABOUT A CURRICULUM-DRIVEN APPROACH

Of course, there are plenty of reasons to think that a district-led, curriculum-driven approach to instructional reform might not work and might simply re-create the problems of standards. It is worth spending a bit of time discussing these concerns, both to address them and to raise legitimate issues that would need attention if we pursued a line of reform like this.

One critique of curriculum-driven instructional reform is that we have tried it before and it didn't work. Indeed, from the 1950s to the 1970s, the National Science Foundation (NSF) spent hundreds of millions of dollars to support the creation of curriculum materials, the training of teachers to use those materials, and their implementation in classrooms around the country.[20] The consensus view of those efforts is that they did little to meaningfully change instruction at scale.[21] While the new materials were praised for the content they included as compared with the materials they replaced, there was very limited evidence to suggest major changes in teacher practice or student outcomes.[22] And while these materials were fairly widely adopted (evidence suggests 30–40 percent of schools adopted one of the NSF materials at their peak, though data on textbook adoption has always been spotty), many of the materials seemed to sit on teachers' shelves unused. Instead, the curriculum reforms fell victim to commonly understood problems—lack of sufficient teacher training exacerbated by the rather large changes in instruction called for by the materials, excessive modification of the adopted materials in ways that contradicted their intent, and fear of a national curriculum, among others. When the federal support for these programs dried up, they all but went away.[23]

While this history is important to remember and learn from, there are many ways in which the lessons of the curriculum-driven reform efforts of the 1970s are not as relevant as they seem. One reason is because the surrounding policy context today is more supportive of these kinds of instructional reforms than that of the 1970s. In that era, curriculum was used in a context with little other instructional guidance—no state standards or assessments, for instance. Now, curriculum-driven reform operates in a system where it is taken as a given that the state has an appropriate role in specifying what students are to know and be able to do. In that era, the reform was especially driven by the NSF, a federal agency, so concerns about a national curriculum were paramount. It is also worth remembering that at that time there was not even a US Department of Education, so any federal activity in education was quite out of the ordinary. Now, we not only have a US Department of Education that is actively involved in making instructional policy, we have something approaching national standards in mathematics and ELA (though not without their own controversy) and even considerable progress in science. States are also very actively involved in instruction, assessment, and accountability decisions in ways that they certainly were not in the 1960s and 1970s. Some states are even leading the way on the issue of curriculum already. And finally, the quality of educational data, research, and the connection of research to policy and practice is certainly stronger than it was in the 1970s, though of course there is still a long way to go to bring research to bear on teaching and learning. Data and research can inform ongoing improvements to policy and practice in ways now that simply could not have been done in the 1970s.

Relatedly, some might argue that standards haven't really worked and therefore it makes little sense to double down on a curriculum-driven approach that is essentially standards on steroids. This critique falls short in that the architects of the standards movement were, as I wrote earlier, broadly correct in their critiques of US education. We do have wide-scale problems with the content of instruction and with the distribution of quality instruction according to student characteristics. But if you believe that the problems are real then surely the governments that fund and run K–12 schools should do something to try to solve them. What other approach is proposed to deal with the problem of low-quality and highly unequal teaching and learning? School reform models like school choice (public or private) can work in some places but clearly cannot get the job done at scale.[24] Indeed, they fall victim to some of the same issues—yes, there are shining examples of high-performing charter schools, but the average effect of school choice on student outcomes is very close to zero. School funding reforms do boost student learning but have nothing to say about what goes on inside classrooms, and these are expensive (though cost-effective) and seem to work best in places where there is also results-oriented accountability.[25] More community-driven local control approaches emphasizing democratic engagement have similarly failed repeatedly, so there's little reason to think devolving that authority back to localities will lead to large-scale improvement.[26] Strengthening our approach to teaching and learning through curriculum and intensive professional support is the clearest path forward if we think instruction matters.

Another critique of a curriculum-driven approach to instructional reform is that it is just an effort to strip teachers' authority even more than it already has been stripped. A different variant on this critique is that curriculum-driven reform is an attempt to "teacher proof" the classroom. There are a few ways in which this argument falls short. First, teachers make clear that, by and large, they want a good core curriculum. I have already presented this evidence. They do not want to be told what to do in a scripted way that actually does take their autonomy away, but they do want to have materials they can rely on to off-load some of the responsibility of delivering a quality curriculum.[27] This is likely especially true for certain kinds of teachers—teachers new to the profession or those new to a given grade or subject, as well as elementary teachers who must teach multiple subjects.[28] Second, there is nothing in the ideas described so far that strips teacher authority. Rather, the model redirects teacher authority away from curriculum selection and curation—something that is time-consuming and difficult, that they are not trained in, and that contributes to inequities in student opportunity—and toward curriculum implementation. Teachers in our case study districts that had this kind of approach to curriculum expressed more satisfaction with the support they were receiving and with their jobs in general; they did not long for the days when they spent hours searching Teachers Pay Teachers.

It is worth mentioning here that there are many instances of truly scripted curriculum used in schools. Two of the most prominent examples are Success For All and Open Court Reading, but even the popular EngageNY contains enough teacher guidance that it might be considered scripted. In practice, the difference between a scripted curriculum and one that contains high-quality teacher guidance is probably more about the expectations for teacher use than it is about the curriculum itself. That is, EngageNY can be delivered in a setting where it might actually be considered scripted—where school leaders make clear to teachers that they are expected to follow the lesson scripts provided—but in the large majority of school settings it is clearly not scripted because teachers report that they extensively modify and supplement it.[29] Furthermore, I am categorically not suggesting that schools adopt policies or practice that even approach scripting. Rather, the argument is that trying to implement standards without a comprehensive core curriculum that is well supported is a waste of time and energy, because it has not worked in the past and will not work in the future. Thus, materials must be a central part of instructional reform efforts or those efforts are not worth pursuing.

A fourth critique might be that curricular standardization is bad for students, so rather than doubling down on instructional reform through curriculum we should abandon it altogether and leave it to local educators to decide what and how to teach students. For instance, standards critics often rail against a one-size-fits-all approach to teaching and learning on the grounds that it does not reflect divergent student needs. But this argument presumes that centralized curriculum adoption has anything at all to do with differentiation of instruction for student needs, which it need not. A strong core curriculum may actually be more suited to differentiation, because giving a teacher these materials reduces teacher workload in selecting materials; they can redirect that workload toward differentiation.

Another argument here is that core curriculum materials are not culturally relevant to diverse learners.[30] But again there is no reason that this must be so—a state could and should approve core curriculum materials that are relevant for diverse learners in the state, and districts could support teachers to collaboratively supplement core materials that enhance their cultural relevance. That curriculum reforms in the past may have been implemented in ways that reduce cultural relevance does not mean that all curriculum reform efforts are by definition counter to cultural relevance. In fact, well-chosen and thoughtfully designed core materials can be highly culturally relevant, and their creators can learn from implementation and improve cultural relevance over time in ways that make it more likely to achieve at scale. For instance, Louisiana has improved its Guidebooks over time to boost its relevance to Black and ELL students in the state.[31] Building cultural relevance into a core curriculum is very likely a more effective way to ensure students have access to a culturally relevant curriculum than relying on individual teachers to construct that relevance themselves.

THE GRAND BARGAIN

The trade-off offered here is a simple one. Standards implementation that is divorced from curriculum is not working, so we should lead with curriculum instead. Teachers should be given high-quality core materials that they are expected to actually use. In exchange for this, which does strip some degree of teachers' authority over one area of their work, teachers should be given greater supports to collaboratively work with colleagues to implement the materials, to learn what is working and what is not for their students, and to modify and supplement in ways that enhance the core curriculum, not detract from it. There are more elements to my ideal teaching reforms, which I will bring up in the next two chapters, but even doing just this would lead to individual districts seeing important improvements in the quality and coherence of their instruction that would benefit kids.

CHAPTER 7

The Imperative for State Leadership in Instructional Reform

If we can agree that improving instruction at scale is a worthy goal, and if I have convinced you that this can be accomplished only through the adoption and use of high-quality core curriculum materials, then the next question is how do we get these materials from the publishers' printing presses (or the coders' monitors) into teachers' hands? Answering that question is the focus of this chapter.

While the previous chapter focused mainly on teachers and districts, this chapter focuses on states. States have considerable control and responsibility over the provision of education in the United States. And while they could use this authority to try to rein in school districts' curriculum-related policies and practices, they mostly have not done so. They have fallen back on "local control" or arguments about "this is how it has always been done" to avoid taking serious responsibility in this area. The truth is that only states are well positioned to encourage widespread instructional improvement through curriculum materials. Individual districts can of course effect change as well, but with more than thirteen thousand districts nationwide this is hardly a path to any kind of curricular standardization or quality. The chapter is organized from least to most ambitious in scope and starts with a summary of some of the evidence discussed previously, with a focus on the successful reforms in Louisiana.

THE IMPERATIVE FOR STATE LEADERSHIP

In May of 2000, the American Civil Liberties Union (ACLU), Public Advocates, the Mexican American Legal Defense Fund, and other civil rights organizations filed a class-action lawsuit against the state of California on behalf of public school students.[1] The lawsuit argued that the state, through its public schools, was denying California students their fundamental constitutional right to an education by failing to provide them with adequate textbooks, school facilities, and quality teachers. Sally Chung, in a report published by the ACLU Foundation of Southern California, describes the case:

> The case was premised on two basic principles: 1) The State of California is responsible for ensuring that all students have the basic resources they need to learn—qualified teachers, sufficient textbooks and instructional materials, and decent facilities; and 2) All students have a fundamental right to an education that must be provided to all students on equal terms. The case argued that California's public education system failed on both of these counts: it did not give all students the necessary educational resources and it allowed unequal opportunities to persist across schools.[2]

The case was settled and legislation was enacted in 2004 that guaranteed that all California students had a right to "sufficient textbooks," "a qualified teacher," and a school in "good repair."[3]

Fifteen years after the settlement, there is good reason to believe that the inequities raised in the case have been somewhat reduced. The ACLU reports that the percentage of low-achieving schools with textbook insufficiencies, for instance, declined from 19 percent to 5 percent. Similarly, the percentage of schools with facilities deficiencies declined by 11 percentage points, and the percentage of misassigned teachers was cut in half. Achievement gaps in the state remain large, however—not much smaller than when the law was enacted. And school districts serving disadvantaged students remain considerably more likely to have resource inadequacies, including shortages of qualified teachers, in spite of the law's reporting and accountability requirements.[4]

Williams v. California—and what has happened since—is instructive for a few reasons.[5] First, the *Williams* case rightly identifies the absolute centrality of the teacher and the curriculum to educational reform efforts. In her expert testimony in the case, Jeannie Oakes made this case clearly and forcefully, emphasizing "the critical importance of effective teachers, relevant instructional materials that students may use at school and at home, and clean, safe, and educationally appropriate facilities." She argued that "students who do not receive these inputs suffer reduced educational outcomes, diminished changes to compete for good jobs and economic security, and limited opportunities to participate in civic life."[6] This was true in 2004, and it remains true today—you cannot address performance gaps without addressing teaching and learning through curriculum and teacher quality efforts.

Second, like many other court cases in other states, the *Williams* case and settlement turn on an interpretation that states have the constitutional responsibility to provide not just an education but a minimally adequate educational opportunity. And the *Williams* enforcement mechanisms, targeted as they are at low-performing schools serving low-income and underrepresented students, have clear equity goals as well. Third, the results of the *Williams* case make clear that merely addressing crudely measured inputs—in this case, for curriculum material access and teacher quality—will not accomplish meaningful equity goals. More than a decade after *Williams* the input gaps are considerably reduced, but the outcome gaps persist. The Hispanic-white gap in California fourth-grade math was 27 points in 2000; it is 25 points now. The gap between students who are and are not eligible for the National School Lunch Program in eighth-grade math was 29 points in 2000; it is 36 points now.[7]

ADVICE AND SUPPORT TO SELECT AND IMPLEMENT QUALITY MATERIALS

The least states can do with respect to implementing quality curriculum is offer districts guidance about what materials to adopt and how to implement them. This approach aims to take a solution that is working in some districts—high-quality curriculum driving instructional improvement and student achievement—and scale it up as much as possible to a state level. Remarkably, this low bar is one that many states—perhaps most—cannot currently clear. Even in California, where the *Williams* settlement asserted curriculum materials as necessary for providing an education of minimally sufficient quality, curriculum materials are recommended in only two subjects (math and ELA), and only in grades K–8. Moving to this kind of state-led advisory curriculum approach should include some of the following.

First, all states should be putting out guidance about what curriculum materials are appropriate and aligned with state standards, not just in the core subjects of mathematics and ELA, but in all subjects that the state expects schools to offer and students to take. This guidance might involve states conducting their own reviews of potential materials, or it might involve states leaning on existing reviews (either from other states or from EdReports.org or other external organizations). If states have similar standards, they could work together on these reviews, perhaps supported or organized by organizations like the Council of Chief State School Officers. These reviews should include not just a judgment of whether particular materials are "above the bar" or not, but also detailed feedback about each material's strengths and weaknesses and areas that need remediation if those materials are to be used in schools. The review process should be inclusive, taking in as many of the available materials in the marketplace as possible and evaluating them against clear criteria. Teachers should be heavily involved in the review process, and the training for the reviews should be well documented and extensive. My research with school district leaders about their textbook adoption decisions suggests that their views of the quality of state-approved textbook lists depend to a large extent on how rigorous they think the review process was and how involved teachers were.[8]

Second, the state should not merely indicate whether materials are "good enough" versus "not"—they should put out the details of the actual reviews, including identifying the strengths and weaknesses of each adopted material. Putting out the details of the actual reviews that materials receive would serve several important purposes. For one, it would offer useful information to districts needing to make decisions—they could easily see what state reviewers thought were the benefits and drawbacks of each of the adopted materials, which might allow them to make better, more informed decisions, or at the very least save the effort of reevaluating materials in every district making an adoption decision. For another, it would give the reviews more credibility in the eyes of the educators eventually making those decisions.

Right now, my interviews with district leaders suggest that state adoptions don't pass the smell test for many of them, because states end up endorsing obviously flawed materials (insofar as all materials are seen as flawed in some way or another) as being fully aligned and meeting standards. Indeed, I have heard this from school district leaders who have told me that they were disappointed with the alignment of materials that had passed the state's review process. If instead the state said "these are the materials that are above our quality bar, but each material has its own strengths and weaknesses, which are XYZ," that would go a long way toward convincing educators that the state had done a serious and fair review. In short, state adoptions, where they happen, are a missed opportunity.

Third, states should actively try to fill the holes of materials they have approved for the state list. This kind of work should leverage the review process to identify strengths and weaknesses in each material and build or identify open educational resources to fill those gaps. Even for materials that are well rated, the state can undoubtedly identify additional supports to address common perceived shortcomings of virtually all materials, such as their ability to be differentiated for high- and low-performing students and their appropriateness for culturally diverse students. This work can also happen over time—states can assemble committees of educators who are implementing state-approved materials in their classrooms and who can be tasked with identifying areas of challenge during implementation. Again, these challenge areas can then be addressed and the supports provided more broadly as open educational resources. This kind of strategy from states can help reduce the need for teachers to seek supplementary materials of unknown quality and ensure coherence and consistency in the curriculum.

Fourth, states should at minimum encourage districts to adopt the materials that they review as being sufficiently high quality (otherwise, why conduct the reviews at all?). One strategy for encouraging districts to adopt particular materials is for the state to make it easier or more affordable for districts to adopt that material, perhaps by offering simplified ordering or bulk discounts for materials purchased through the state. Another strategy is for the state to prioritize selecting or offering high-quality materials for free as open educational resources. States can also encourage districts by providing other kinds of supports, such as professional learning, supplemental curriculum resources, or curriculum-aligned formative assessments to districts that adopt materials on the state-approved list. Offering these supports can take some of the burden off district leaders for sourcing curriculum-related supports and can improve the coherence and quality of what teachers are getting.

Fifth, states should try to simplify the adoption process for districts, which is currently quite burdensome. This kind of support could take several forms. One form is simply to provide better data on the strengths and weaknesses of various materials, as discussed above. Rather than encouraging districts to conduct their own alignment analyses of available materials, as many states currently do, states should conduct clear and high-quality alignment analyses and make those data available. Indeed, the state should probably discourage districts from duplicating work that state committees have already done—there is little reason to think that individual districts could do a better job than a well-trained group of educators at the state level. Additionally, states could support districts by putting out guidance for what a textbook adoption process should look like. This guidance should be simplified and streamlined, cutting out extraneous steps like school board votes that should have no bearing on educators' informed decisions. It could include suggestions for piloting and aggregating results from pilots and could be drawn from processes that are already in place and updated routinely. Furthermore, states could encourage districts that are near each other (geographically or in terms of student composition) to make joint adoption decisions. Joint adoption decisions can encourage consistency, lead to greater opportunities for collaboration, and support mobile students or students in areas with high degrees of educational choice.

Last, all states should at minimum collect data on what materials are adopted in each school and district. California attempted this as part of the *Williams* settlement, but their efforts were fraught with problems, especially missing or unclear data but also the complete lack of interest among members of the public to hold schools accountable for the provision of these key resources (as specified in the theory of action underlying the settlement).[9] I have written elsewhere about challenges in even collecting and disseminating usable textbook data, but here are some of the high-level highlights.[10] States should routinize the collection of textbook data at the time materials are purchased or adopted, rather than attempting to gather these data via surveys (unless those surveys are mandatory and very well designed to provide the needed information). States should standardize the ways in which textbook adoption data, such as titles, publishers, and adoption years, are recorded. States should strategize about what to collect from districts that say they are not adopting any formal curriculum. In California this is around 5 percent of districts in the core subjects, though many more than 5 percent of teachers report using teacher-created materials. After all, it is not as if districts that do not adopt a material should be exempt from any kind of curriculum oversight! States should make the data publicly available so that districts can use the data to build collaborations and other stakeholders can know what materials are available in schools. And finally, rather than assuming the data will get used by some imaginary public body (which has never yet materialized in states that have collected these data), states should build partnerships with researchers to conduct planned analyses on questions they care about.[11]

In many states, the state does not even do any of these activities. Rather than supporting districts by providing them with more information about available materials, these states leave districts on their own to evaluate materials, make adoption decisions, and support teacher implementation. Is it any surprise that district adoption processes are onerous and require substantial duplicative work that still results in many students having no core materials or materials that are of questionable quality? Is it any surprise that in most states we actually have no idea at all what materials are adopted by districts, let alone used by teachers? These are all areas that we can address relatively easily through a slightly more assertive state role that would not in any way infringe upon districts' control over the materials they adopt and encourage teachers to use.

THE SPECIAL CASE OF STATE-CREATED CURRICULA

It may be that some state leaders look at the available curriculum options and decide that there are insufficient high-quality options available. Or it may be that state leaders see high-quality options but feel strongly that there also needs to be a locally developed or locally relevant option. In that case, states can certainly work with educators and publishers to create high-quality materials that they can then include on the recommended textbook list. There are already two prominent and successful examples for states to draw on—New York's EngageNY and Louisiana's Guidebooks. The development and dissemination of these materials are already described in depth elsewhere, but here I briefly highlight some of the lessons of these two efforts for other states that wish to develop their own materials.

EngageNY is an open educational resource material created by the New York State Department of Education using Race to the Top funds. It is a full curriculum for K–12 ELA and mathematics and is written to align with the Common Core standards (to which it has a fully aligned rating from EdReports). Because New York is a local control state when it comes to curriculum, the state has made sure to emphasize that EngageNY is optional and flexible: "In order to assist educators with the implementation of the Common Core, the New York State Education Department provides curricular modules in P–12 English Language Arts and Mathematics that schools and districts can adopt or adapt for local purposes."[12] EngageNY mathematics is also published by Great Minds in a more traditional form as Eureka Math. EngageNY ELA is published by four different publishing companies, depending on grade.

A recent report by researchers at RAND described the prevalence of EngageNY and explored why it is popular with teachers.[13] For starters, it is a widely used material—evidence suggests it is especially so in New York, but it is also one of the most commonly used curriculum materials around the country (it is even used by some teachers in non–Common Core states). According to nationally representative American Teacher Panel data, EngageNY was the most widely used material in elementary mathematics, the fifth most widely used material in secondary mathematics, the fifth most widely used specific material in elementary ELA, and the fourth most widely used specific material in secondary ELA.[14] Teachers use the material both as a resource and as a full curriculum. There is some evidence that ELA teachers are more likely to do the latter than mathematics teachers, but with many teachers indicating they use the material daily or often.

Teachers offer a variety of reasons for the use of EngageNY, which are instructive for efforts to get materials to be used more widely. Of course, a main driver of usage is the expectations of schools and districts—teachers use the materials more if they are required or suggested to by their leaders than if they are finding them on their own. This is a seemingly minor point, but it does actually matter what recommendations and requirements districts make, even if teachers are far from perfect in their adherence to district curriculum expectations. Teachers also report using EngageNY because they perceive it to be high quality and well aligned with Common Core standards (which reviews from EdReports suggest is true). Interestingly, very few teachers cited the freely available nature of EngageNY as a major reason they used it. In short, EngageNY seems to be quite successful at getting adopted and used by teachers, both in New York and around the country, and that success seems to be driven more by its quality and alignment, as well as district expectations, than by its availability as an open educational resource.

Louisiana's Guidebooks offer another interesting case study of state-created curriculum materials. I already discussed their strategy in earlier chapters, but a few points are worth emphasizing here as pertains to the state role. One important point is that the Guidebooks arose out of the state's perception of a gap in the available materials. To be sure, many materials exist that are well rated by EdReports, but state leaders there still felt that a new option was needed, so they created one. Another key point is that the state didn't just create a material and put it out into the universe; rather, they set up state policies to encourage districts to adopt the material and they continue to support teachers to use the material in desired ways. A third key point is that the materials are seen as a work in progress rather than a static object—the state has already revised the materials twice, each time deepening the materials in important ways called for by the state's educators.

I firmly do not believe that we need fifty states creating core curriculum materials in each subject, especially when many good materials already exist and large numbers of states share standards. That said, for state leaders who believe that state control of curriculum is important, New York and Louisiana offer important models of possible approaches to the creation and dissemination of materials. Given how widely used these materials are, both in their respective states and elsewhere, this seems like a promising approach. In neither case has the use of these materials been mandated, yet the market has clearly signaled that they view the materials as high quality and worth using. State-led creation of materials should continue to be supported, perhaps by grants from the federal government or from philanthropies. The story of EngageNY and the Guidebooks suggests that such an approach would likely have a major impact on the kinds of materials that are adopted and ultimately used, even without new mandates.

ASSERTING A MORE ACTIVE STATE ROLE

What I've proposed so far is a modest but important variant on what a small number of states are already doing. If all states did these things—conduct comprehensive reviews, recommend and support certain materials they rate as high quality, and create new materials where there are gaps in the existing market—this would be a tremendous step forward that would get many more districts to adopt high-quality materials and therefore expose millions more children to higher-quality curriculum than they're currently getting. But it would be well within states' power, and I believe well worth the political effort it would require, for state departments of education to go one step further than this and simply mandate that schools and districts adopt one of the approved curricula. Or, to put it another way, it would be well within states' power—and clearly in the best interests of students—if the state department of education prohibited public school districts from using curriculum materials that it evaluated as being of inferior quality.

It goes almost without saying that states are well within their authority to mandate particular curricula. The federal government clearly does not have this authority:

> No provision of any applicable program shall be construed to authorize any department, agency, officer, or employee of the United States to exercise any direction, supervision, or control over the curriculum, program of instruction, administration, or personnel of any educational institution, school, or school system, or over the selection of library resources, textbooks, or other printed or published instructional materials by any educational institution or school system.[15]

But state governments do have authority over the provision of education, including issues related to curriculum. And while no states currently mandate any particular curriculum materials, the most ambitious state policies at present are still advisory.

There are several reasons why states should consider mandating that districts use one of a few core materials. The first is that, almost by definition, this will result in better-quality materials being used, on average, in the state. If the state sets up a good review process that it believes accurately captures materials' quality, then requiring districts to use one of the chosen materials will guarantee that all students will have access to a high-quality material. In contrast, an advisory-only policy, as is currently the most ambitious state policy, will result in some schools choosing nonadvised materials, including creating their own, and these will likely be of lesser quality (certainly any material that was evaluated by the state and seen as not good enough to recommend must be considered of lower quality).

The second is that mandating that districts adopt from one of a small number of approved materials means that the state can support districts more directly. Louisiana demonstrates the possibilities that come when a large majority of districts are using a single curriculum. For instance, this means that the state can provide professional development specifically focused on that curriculum. It can also infuse curriculum-specific learning into preservice teacher education. The state could also create or source supplements, which could be locally relevant or culturally appropriate for the state's students, to address shortcomings of adopted materials. The state could also create or propose well-aligned interim or benchmark assessment systems that schools and districts could choose to adopt. The state could ensure its teacher evaluation policies were better aligned with the available curriculum as well. Our recent work on coherent policy systems finds that teachers are often operating in environments where key policy features— standards, curriculum materials, assessments, teacher evaluation, and the like—are lacking. Just about a quarter of teachers in Massachusetts and Rhode Island had policy contexts that we classified as coherent.[16] In contrast, by narrowing districts' curricular options with a focus on quality and supporting those options centrally, Louisiana got about three-quarters of its teachers to be located in coherent policy systems. Going just one step further than Louisiana and mandating districts adopt from among a small list of approved materials would undoubtedly increase policy coherence even more.

How many materials should states allow districts to choose from? I don't think there's a magic number, but the simple truth is that there can be economies of scale in supporting implementation only if there are just a few widely used options in a state. Louisiana, for instance, currently rates two to six materials as Tier 1 standards-aligned, depending on subject and grade level. Somewhere in this range seems reasonable, but more than six materials would start to make the adoption prevalence too diffuse for the state to be able to support the materials much.

Would state mandates for districts to choose from among a fairly limited set of approved materials infringe to some extent on districts' authority to make curricular decisions? That is one way of thinking about this kind of approach, yes. A different way of thinking about it is that there is no obvious reason why districts should have this authority in the first place. It is the state that has the responsibility to provide an education, not the district—school districts are, after all, creations of the state. That the state has always chosen to devolve authority over curriculum to the district does not mean it must always be so. Further, it is not at all obvious that school districts are best positioned to make curricular decisions. Districts have made these decisions for years, and many of the decisions that they have made seem not to have resulted in improvements in educational opportunities for children. They have often adopted poorly aligned materials, or sometimes no materials at all, and these problems have been especially severe in districts serving more disadvantaged students. Indeed, this was the rationale for the *Williams* lawsuit and settlement! Furthermore, there are much larger within-district differences than between-district differences in performance, so arguments that districts' students are so unique that they cannot possibly adopt the materials adopted by other districts across the state ring more than a little hollow.[17]

If anything, what the *Williams* settlement (and other recent court cases on related topics, such as lawsuits about a "right to literacy") suggests is that the state should take more responsibility for ensuring the provision of a quality education to all children.[18] It does not make sense to, on the one hand, state that the content in standards or curriculum is essential content that every child should learn and then, on the other hand, take few efforts to ensure that students are even being taught that content. The most direct step the state could take to begin to assert its responsibility for the quality of education is to require certain minimum standards of quality, including the adoption of strong curriculum materials. The indirect approach of using test scores to shine a light on underperformance is simply not working well enough to drive change.

MOVING BEYOND ADOPTION

Of course, the elephant in the room when it comes to curriculum is that adoption is only a very small part of the battle of getting good content taught to students. Virtually all teachers modify and supplement, and it is really what they deliver to students that matters. While there is very compelling evidence that individual curriculum materials do differ in their impacts on student learning, any state policy that stops at adoption will have at best a modest effect on teaching and learning.[19] Getting beyond adoption to implementation is incredibly thorny, but this chapter concludes with a few thoughts about how states can encourage better implementation and get a handle on what's being implemented, where, and how.

Implementation of curriculum materials is so weak to some extent because teachers think the adopted materials are inappropriate for their students or just not very good. So, one answer to the question of how to drive better implementation is for the core materials to be better. A centralized state adoption should result in better materials on average for all the reasons discussed above, but that will make only a small dent in supplementation and modification, as survey research makes clear. Research from Louisiana does suggest that teachers there are supplementing less than teachers in other states, perhaps in part because they have stronger, more relevant core material and are receiving better support on implementing it.[20] But these differences are not huge, and there is still a great deal of supplementation going on in Louisiana classrooms.

The kinds of strategies discussed above should also reduce supplementation to some extent. For instance, if the state identifies gaps in the adopted materials and selects or creates supplementals to fill those gaps, that could drive supplementation to at least be largely using approved materials. If the state provides high-quality professional learning focused on the adopted materials, as Louisiana does, that could encourage better implementation— if teachers better understand the instructional vision of the adopted materials, that may make them more inclined to use those materials and in ways intended by the materials' authors. Another strategy that should improve implementation is to more tightly align other policy instruments with the state's approved curriculum materials. Key possibilities here include teacher evaluation and interim assessments. If the protocols that were used in teacher evaluation were curriculum-linked—if they reinforced the instructional vision and organization of the core curriculum materials and gauged teachers' implementation of those materials—they would certainly reinforce the message that teachers should be using the materials. If the state recommended or provided curriculum-aligned interim assessments that supported appropriate pacing of the adopted curriculum, that would similarly encourage more coherent implementation (and also provide teachers with evidence about how well students were mastering the curriculum).

Finally, states that actually want to encourage curriculum implementation and quality instruction should consider whether they should engage in measurement efforts to try to ensure students have access to those things. Certainly aligning the structure of teacher evaluations with curriculum materials would enable some level of evaluation of curriculum implementation. But states might also either conduct or task others with conducting periodic curriculum audits, especially in schools where student achievement growth is lagging and in schools that do not choose to adopt core materials that are approved by the state as high quality. These audits would not need to be intrusive. They could involve surveying teachers or parents about the curriculum materials that are available and used. Or they could involve review of documents submitted by teachers or school leaders describing their enacted curriculum. There are a variety of tools and processes that already exist; there is no need to reinvent the wheel. These audits could go a long way toward ensuring that students have access to an enacted curriculum that is high quality and that is aligned with state expectations. They could also be formative and offer teachers or district curriculum leaders the opportunity to learn about ways to improve curriculum implementation and instruction.

Regardless of the specific approach taken, the important consideration is that states have the authority and the obligation to ensure that students have access to a quality education. Curriculum is at the heart of the educational opportunity that schools and districts provide, and therefore it should be central in states' oversight and support efforts. There is a continuum of control that states can exert over the curriculum decisions of local educators. Being farther along on that continuum—more prescriptive on the kinds of materials districts should adopt, and more supportive of the understanding and implementation of those materials—is an important path forward for states that wish to really move the needle on instruction.

CHAPTER 8

When Everyone's in Charge, Is Anyone in Charge?

In early 2020, as I was writing this book, the world was gripped by the COVID-19 pandemic. By all accounts, the United States failed spectacularly in its response to the crisis as compared with virtually any other nation on earth. We failed on testing and tracing, leading to repeated waves of breakouts that roiled the economy throughout the year and led to the deaths of over 400,000 Americans. We failed on masking, with right-wing media and an unhinged president fueling a dangerous antimask movement (after initial failures on masking from the Centers for Disease Control and Prevention and World Health Organization) and pushing COVID treatments demonstrated to be ineffective in multiple clinical studies. And we failed on education, putting far too much effort into planning for in-person reopening and far too little effort planning for how to deliver online instruction as effectively as possible.

There are so many indicators of our educational failures during the COVID pandemic. Here are a few that are relevant to the point I want to make in this final chapter.

The Center on Reinventing Public Education (CRPE) at the University of Washington analyzed state plans and rules with regard to school reopening in late July of 2020, just three to six weeks from the start of the school year in most places and more than three months after the first wave of the virus engulfed the nation.[1] They found that states had left many consequential reopening decisions up to school districts and sometimes not even exercised authority over reopening plans. For instance, only fifteen states required districts to have remote learning plans for reopening and only half of states required a reopening plan at all. Even in the states where districts required plans, they almost never required any specific educational activities other than some minimum amount of contact hours or attendance taking. They certainly didn't offer specific advice about how to teach K–12 students in a largely online format or how to adapt or select curriculum for that purpose, something that virtually all K–12 educators have not been trained to do. Rather than laying out clear expectations for what teaching and learning should look like in the pandemic, offering districts supports like quality online curriculum materials to implement those expectations, or even planning to track the educational impact of COVID through formative assessments, states mostly devolved responsibility for responding to the crisis to thirteen thousand district leaders and school boards.

It might not surprise you to know that school districts were not well prepared to deliver quality instruction, either. A study from June of 2020, also conducted by CRPE, found that just one-third of school district plans in a national sample required teachers to deliver live instruction to all students.[2] There were substantial gaps based on school district demographics, with significantly more affluent districts and districts in urban and suburban areas requiring live instruction as compared with more rural districts or those serving more low-income students. Just under half of districts required teachers to track student engagement through attendance or check-ins. Research from Brookings suggested that school district reopening plans were not driven by local differences in the threat of the virus; rather, they were driven by partisan politics. Districts where more voters supported Donald Trump in 2016 were substantially more likely to have plans emphasizing in-person instruction, and those that were more Democratic were more likely to emphasize remote learning.[3] States passed the buck to districts, and district plans (or the lack thereof) made it clear that districts were not the right level to be making difficult decisions about reopening, teaching, and learning in the time of the pandemic. This is not because the educators in those districts were inadequate in some way; it's because they did not have expertise in delivering online learning in a pandemic because that had never been provided to them before.

You might think that these are just plans, and what actually matters is what students experienced in the digital classroom. To some extent you'd be right—it's certainly possible to deliver a quality learning experience in spite of a complete lack of preparation and support. But that doesn't seem to be how it's panned out. The differences in educational experiences under COVID-19 went far beyond plans. Surveys from the American Institutes for Research found sharp differences between more and less affluent school districts in the nature of the instruction they provided.[4] About a third of low-income districts reported primarily emphasizing review of content taught during the early part of the pandemic, versus just 8 percent of more affluent districts. About half of low-income districts reported distributing paper packets of materials for students to use, while more affluent districts overwhelmingly relied on digital materials. These differences in digital instruction are not surprising; a nationally representative survey that I co-directed, the Understanding America Study, found a vast digital divide at the start of the pandemic, with just 63 percent of the lowest-income Americans having access to a computer and internet to do schoolwork at home.[5]

Of course, districts cannot be expected to solve inequities in students' incomes and associated factors such as technology and internet access—this is a job for actors at a higher level, like states working with the federal government. Neither can districts be expected to find the funds to support the extra costs associated with teaching in the time of COVID—states and districts, which are the primary funders of education, have been under tremendous financial strain and simply do not have the ability to create the funds necessary to fill budget gaps. And these results and others show that there are enormous differences across districts—differences correlated with where the districts are located and what kinds of children they serve—in responses to the pandemic and in the ability to provide quality instruction remotely. Again, districts are not the right level of authority to address these gaps—states or the federal government are. But that is not what we saw during the early response to the COVID crisis, and the result has been, by all accounts, a nearly unmitigated educational disaster.

This is not a book about COVID-19, but the crisis illustrates several important facts that are relevant to the argument I want to make in the final chapter of the book. The argument in this chapter is that teaching and learning is far from the only area in which our antiquated local control approach to governing schools gets in the way of both equity and excellence in American education. During the COVID crisis this has been laid completely bare. School district leaders are not public health experts. Leaving critical decisions about how to safely provide instruction in the time of the pandemic to school district leaders accomplishes two things—it burdens these leaders tremendously, forcing them to spend hours making decisions they are neither trained nor supported to make, and it decreases the likelihood that decisions will be made on the best available evidence.[6] Of course, state leaders in some states have also made decisions that run counter to the best available evidence, in some cases even overruling local actors who wanted to make the right choices. So more centralized control is not a panacea. But local control in this case is all but guaranteed to exacerbate inequality and burden educators.

The pandemic will eventually end, and fifty million children will go back to thirteen thousand school districts. Learning will probably return largely to normal. But that's not good enough if the goal is preparing students to achieve success in college or the workforce, and it's not good enough if the goal is closing long-standing outcome gaps in education. If students return to the system they left, little will change, and we will all be worse off for it.

OUR STRUCTURAL FLAWS

Much has been written about the governance challenges in American education.[7] And it is worth starting this discussion by acknowledging that we are neither Singapore nor Finland, and we never will be. We are a highly diverse nation with long-standing educational structures and a history of local and state control in education. At most, we could be fifty Singapores, but even that would be a monumental change from where we are now. So, what I am arguing for in this book is not national control of education. It is not national standards, national textbooks, or even national teacher certification requirements. It is not a national school board, nor a national school czar in the US Department of Education. All of those things are impossible.

I'm not so sure they'd be worse than what we have now, but they're off the table. What's on the table, though, is much more radical change led by the fifty states.

The question I set out to answer in this book is, "What would it take for every child in American public schools to receive a high-quality education?" We could answer this question with a few bullet points—what we could agree on as the fundamental elements of a good education. These would include the same sorts of things called for by Smith and O'Day thirty years ago—things like the following, at minimum:

- High-quality teachers who provide excellent instruction to all students
- A challenging, content-rich curriculum that prepares students to succeed beyond school in college or the workforce
- Necessary academic and nonacademic supports such as special education, English language instruction, and social-emotional learning
- Safe and supportive school environments free from racial and other forms of bias

There are probably other elements, too, but this is the lowest bar we might hope our education systems could pass.[8]

The truth is that all of these elements are thwarted to varying degrees by the educational governance systems we have in place today. And as long as we accept the systems as they are—rather than challenging structural elements that lower the quality of education and contribute to widening, rather than narrowing, opportunity gaps—even the most ambitious education policies will not achieve their goals. These structures are many, and they exist both inside and outside the public school system. But they must be dismantled and rebuilt if there is to be large-scale improvement.

I could start my critique of educational governance at any level, but I'll pick the school district because it is the clearest barrier to equity and excellence.[9] Why are there over thirteen thousand school districts in the United States?[10] How did we settle on that number, and is it the right one? There used to be many more—one hundred twenty thousand at the start of World War II, seventy thousand before *Brown v. Board of Education*—but by about 1970 we approached our current number and have lost only about half a percent per year since then. Why did we stop there? The median school district enrollment is a little over eleven hundred students, and about 85 percent of all districts have enrollments below five thousand, so while we might spend a lot of time and energy talking about big urban districts, the vast majority of districts are quite small.[11] Even if we cut to just a district per county (as they do in Florida and most of the South), that would drop our number of districts by about 80 percent, down to around three thousand.

Why should we care about the number of school districts? I have already laid out the case that district leadership in areas of curriculum has resulted in neither equity nor excellence. But the failures of our local-control governance systems extend far beyond curriculum. The organization EdBuild lays out the stark reality of the ways that school districts contribute to racial and socioeconomic inequality and undermine educational excellence. For instance, they document over one thousand school district boundaries that dramatically exacerbate segregation, with students on one side whiter, wealthier, and receiving more dollars per pupil than those on the other side.[12] Thanks to the Supreme Court's ruling in *Milliken v. Bradley*, these district boundaries act as impermeable barriers to educational opportunity. EdBuild describes over one hundred school districts that have seceded from neighboring districts in the last twenty years, almost always for the purpose of an affluent or whiter community fencing itself off from a more diverse district.[13] Remarkably, laws in many states make it downright easy for districts to create these arbitrary barriers that disadvantage those left behind. EdBuild lists the fifty most segregating school district borders, almost all of them in Rust Belt, Northeastern, or Deep South states with tiny districts.[14] Small school districts are a tool of racial segregation—district boundaries are in fact a primary source of segregation in American schools.[15] Through this path, they are a major contributor to educational inequity through their effects on resource gaps that systematically favor majority-white districts.[16]

There are other ways that school districts cause problems beyond merely segregating our students. School district boundaries lead to inequalities in housing prices and appreciation, furthering racial and class gaps in wealth (these findings also apply for school catchment area boundaries, as anyone who has ever looked at real estate listings in a city with schools that vary in levels of perceived quality already knows).[17] School district boundaries, coupled with teacher preferences, exacerbate teacher quality gaps and teacher shortages that disadvantage urban and rural districts and districts serving more low-income students of color.[18] Districts also act to fragment all types of education policies enacted at higher levels. Thirteen thousand districts means there are thirteen thousand different instructional policies, thirteen thousand different approaches to serving students with disabilities and English language learners, thirteen thousand strategies for assessing student progress, thirteen thousand approaches to college and vocational preparation, and thirteen thousand expectations for teacher professional learning.

School districts come with school boards that set their policies and hire their superintendents. The idea of school boards is alluring as a tool for local control and democratic governance. In principle, locally elected boards could be more responsive to local needs—under the assumption that local needs actually vary a lot and in ways that couldn't be accounted for at a higher level—than more centrally administered approaches. Local control could facilitate accountability, offering parents and citizens the opportunity to hold local leaders to task for improved educational outcomes. And locally elected school boards could serve as important launching-off points for public servants from marginalized groups. The reality of school boards (and democratic engagement in education more generally) is far from this vision.[19]

A variety of evidence points to the failure of school boards as tools of democratic engagement or local control. The following are just a few examples:

- Few elections for school board positions are competitive. Surveys of school board members find that just 6 percent describe their elections as "very difficult," as compared with 44 percent who describe their elections as "very easy."[20] Voter turnout in school board elections is vanishingly small, and the voters who do participate are likely to be interest group members who are more advantaged along multiple dimensions.[21] The majority of voters in school board elections do not even have children who attend these local schools, and majority-white electorates select school boards in more than two-thirds of majority-nonwhite school districts.[22]
- Candidates who run for school boards are wealthier and whiter than the population of students they represent.[23] Because so many school

board races are noncompetitive, this means elected school board officials are not representative of the districts they serve.

- There is little evidence that voters hold school board members elector-
ally accountable for student performance when report cards make performance data available.[24] One exception may be when such elections
take place during presidential elections (i.e., when turnout is higher).[25]

Perhaps most worrying is recent evidence that not only are all of the above
true but also the unrepresentativeness of school boards is systematically
related to other outcomes. For instance, the larger the gap between the racial
demographics of the school board and that of its students, the larger the
racial achievement gap in the district.[26] School board demographic composition also affects the demographic composition of the administrators they
hire.[27] And the political composition of school boards affects the policies
they pursue (with more conservative school boards implementing policies
that exacerbate segregation).[28]

The last several years have seen a resurgence of progressive politics on
issues of civil rights, healthcare, criminal justice, and other policy topics.
In education, this progressive turn has trained its focus on attacking school
choice and school discipline programs and building up the possibilities of
community school models. And while these may be worthy targets of our
progressive reform efforts, the powerful role of school districts and school
boards in contributing to racial and socioeconomic equality have been
almost completely sidestepped. A truly progressive agenda for improving
America's schools would question the role of school districts and school
boards in exacerbating racial and socioeconomic inequality and attempt to
use the power of the state to bring about more distributive justice in education. We cannot achieve equity at scale with thirteen thousand school districts operating at current levels of independence from the state that funds
their existence. It is impossible.

SOME PROPOSITIONS FOR A BETTER SYSTEM

Of course it is not just school districts that are problematic and contribute to
fragmentation and incoherence. We could just as easily target our critiques
at any of the other bodies that are involved in education policy, from state

boards of education to county offices of education, from philanthropies to the research community, from teacher education programs to accreditation boards. There are flaws up and down the structure of American educational governance systems. If we were building a new system from scratch—if we didn't have hundreds of years of history, law, and racism setting problematic precedent—what might such a system look like?

A more equitable system would have to start with greater state control in almost all areas, beginning with funding. Since about half of education dollars typically come from local revenues, states that do not equalize those revenues through a progressive funding formula leave low-income districts at a funding disadvantage. While funding equity would require disadvantaged districts to receive *more* educational dollars than districts serving wealthier students, recent evidence shows that this is the case in only a small handful of states.[29] Court-ordered school finance reforms that mandate state involvement in school funding have led to substantial increases in student achievement and narrowing of achievement gaps.[30] When it comes to funding, local control just won't work. States that have not already made investments to raise their funding levels and provide more resources to disadvantaged districts should do so. They can look to states that have done this work successfully—New Jersey is a prime example, though it has taken a long time to get to a place where it is a national leader in funding schools adequately and equitably, and it has backtracked somewhat after recent economic crises.[31]

Why should we stop at school funding, though? There are numerous other ways that state governance structures get in the way of educational equity, some of which I've already touched on above. For instance, teachers are inequitably distributed within and between school districts.[32] Those inequities are on observable measures such as experience and credentials, but also on unobserved measures such as effectiveness as judged by value-added methods and even observational measures of instructional quality.[33] Dan Goldhaber and his colleagues put this bluntly:

> In elementary school, middle school, and high school classrooms, virtually every measure of teacher quality we examine—experience, licensure exam scores, and value added—is inequitably distributed across every indicator

of student disadvantage—free/reduced-price lunch status, underrepresented minority, and low prior academic performance.[34]

We have known about the inequitable distribution of teachers for decades, and while we have dabbled around the edges of this problem we have not taken full advantage of the state's role in solving it.[35]

What would it mean to exercise a more progressive state role in raising and equalizing teacher quality? The most straightforward answer is to raise teacher pay overall in places where it is inadequate relative to other professions with similar educational expectations. Statewide salary schedules (with adjustments for cost of living) could accomplish this, or at least set a floor to ensure that teaching is an economically attractive profession. All states have gaps between teachers and similarly educated workers, but these are dramatically larger in some states than others.[36]

But it is not enough to raise pay overall; a more progressive approach would use state funds to provide incentives for teachers to teach in more disadvantaged schools. These kinds of incentives are far from a panacea, but evidence shows that various policies targeted at schools serving more underserved students, such as bonuses for retention, incentives to teach, and programs that forgive teachers' loans, can indeed help attract and retain high-quality teachers in these settings.[37] Since teacher working conditions also matter for keeping high-quality teachers and contribute to teacher quality gaps, programs aimed at improving these working conditions may also help. Some working conditions that seem to matter and that may be especially amenable to state intervention include the quality of school and district leadership and school facilities.[38] Other creative policies have been proposed, such as policies related to the recruitment of talented students to teacher education programs, the placement of students during the student teaching period, and teacher job differentiation programs. The point is not that any of these policies will solve the problem on its own. The point is that teacher quality gaps are a huge problem that only states or the federal government could address but that they largely have not in any sustained way.

It's true that all of the reforms proposed above cost money, and it can be politically difficult to raise taxes to pay for things that are needed to improve education. Courts can offer the cover needed to get this funding work done, but state leaders can also make compelling cases for raising taxes in targeted ways to provide more and better services to families. For instance, large tax cuts for millionaires and billionaires that were passed under President Trump are incredibly unpopular (in addition to being unnecessary and ineffective at driving economic growth) and should be repealed.[39] At the state level (at least prepandemic) there are plenty of examples of states finding ways to raise funds for needed educational services. For instance, California's Proposition 30 successfully passed in 2012, raising sales taxes by a quarter percent and personal income taxes on wealthy Californians by a few percent. This proposition, coupled with the state's new Local Control Funding Formula, brought in billions of new dollars for California's schools and boosted student achievement and graduation rates, especially for low-income students and students of color.[40] Local governments have been successful in convincing voters to raise taxes to pay for early childhood education, and their approaches may be successful at the state level as well.[41] I am not arguing that these decisions are easy, but I am arguing that there are models that exist for convincing voters that it is important to fund schools well.[42]

There are also many reforms we could pursue that wouldn't necessarily cost so much, though they would obviously encounter their own political challenges. For instance, recognizing the ways school district boundaries contribute to inequities and policy implementation struggles, we could consider any range of policies meant to address school districts. We might start from the most obvious—enclaves should not be allowed to secede from other school districts, or if we do allow secessions we could at least require that those secessions not contribute to racial or socioeconomic segregation or weaken the financial standing of the resulting districts (which would probably kill those secessions, since segregation and resource hoarding seem to be the primary factors causing them).

A bolder approach might recognize school districts' roles in segregating students and thwarting state policies and consolidate school districts dramatically. These could be consolidated to counties in states where counties are relevant administrative bodies, or they could be consolidated to match congressional or state legislative districts, or there could be nonpartisan commissions to divide states up. Any of these approaches would decrease segregation and create more opportunities to build policy structures that address educational inequities (e.g., facilitating public school choice or teacher redistribution), since, again, school district boundaries are the primary driver of student segregation. As long as reporting and accountability were still provided at the school level, any kind of consolidation would facilitate efforts to standardize and improve the implementation of state education policies.

There might also be corresponding changes in school board policies. For instance, research makes very clear that school board elections have higher participation rates if they are conducted in on-cycle elections.[43] There is no reason that states couldn't require all such elections to happen on cycle. Every four years on the presidential cycle would likely be best, since that would maximize participation and would lead to terms of sufficient length that would increase the stability of district-level policy making. School board elections could also move away from at-large (e.g., a slate of five board members elected to represent the entire district without respect to geography) to representing particular zones that could be chosen to maximize demographic diversity. Enlarging the number of seats on school boards, which would be easy since the districts would be larger, would also decrease the power associated with any one seat. States might also consider to what degree elected school boards are needed at all, or whether their powers might be narrowed in ways that reduce their ability to thwart policy implementation.

Again, none of these solutions is the one right solution to get greater implementation of instructional policy or to narrow the opportunities for state policies to be derailed under the guise of local control. But clearly our poor performance indicates that we must think outside the box in terms of the kinds of policies we have pursued up until now, and this thinking must start with structural and governance issues. There is simply no way that we can improve our education system to the degree we need while operating within the current structure. If progressives trust federal and state governments to exercise a firm hand in healthcare, regulation of the economy, and civil rights, we should do so in education as well. This starts with curriculum—the core of this book—but it extends to all areas of education policy. Only state and federal governments can equalize opportunity in education, and they can't do it if they let thirteen thousand districts and school boards stand in the way.

EDUCATION CAN'T DO IT ALONE

We also cannot escape the fact that schools cannot solve our inequality problems alone. Schools are not the primary cause of inequality in educational outcomes—income inequality and structural racism are. Thus, while we must pursue an aggressive agenda to improve education, and while I believe that can happen only through improved curriculum and greater state control, there must be equally aggressive efforts to reform out-of-school factors that contribute to inequity. These barriers are too numerous to list, but they include income and wealth inequality, housing affordability, high-quality healthcare for all, racism in policing and criminal justice, and the long-standing consequences of slavery and historical policies that have limited the prospects of Black and Indigenous Americans in particular.

Yes, we must repair our schools. And improving curriculum is the surest path to do so. But if we do not address broader societal issues such as these, repairing schools will move the needle only so far.

SUMMING UP THE ARGUMENT

The standards movement has been around for thirty years. It hasn't achieved its goals of improving instruction and student achievement at scale, and there is no reason to think that any modest tinkering with the policy—improving the tests, aligning teacher evaluation, improving professional learning—will get the job done. The only way to change instruction at scale is to get much closer to the classroom—to get more teachers to have access to good curriculum materials, to offer them high-quality supports to use those materials, and to ensure that, when they need to supplement or modify those materials, they do so in a way that bolsters, rather than undermines, the coherence of the curriculum students receive. In turn, the only way this level of coordination can happen is if states assert considerably more authority and provide considerably more supportive conditions to districts. Even this will not get us all the way to where we need to be, but it will at least be a worthwhile shot. If we are unwilling to attempt this kind of powerful curricular reform, we may as well not bother with the standards charade.

Even if we can get states to actively involve themselves in the curriculum decisions of districts and schools and the provision of support to ensure consistent implementation, the truth is that there are too many other structural barriers that impede educational improvement. Chief among these are the radically decentralized systems that undermine policy and segregate our students. But that is just the tip of the iceberg. There are policies and structures just under the surface that contribute to educational inequity and all but ensure that disadvantaged student groups receive a lower-quality education. Without a major overhaul of these systems, the gains from even a considerable centralization of curriculum authority will likely be modest. In short, our problems are big, so we have to think much bigger than we have been.

Can we afford what needs to be done? Of course we can. This is a question of priorities, not resources. The better question is whether we can afford not to. It's clear that many of the key structures in our society are reaching their breaking point, including our public school systems. There was already tremendous strain on our systems before the COVID-19 pandemic and the reckoning with structural racism in light of the murder of George Floyd. If we cannot emerge from these twin crises with a renewed effort to bring about massive structural change, we will not get another opportunity like this for decades.

Can we muster the political will to do it? This is the more difficult question. There are entrenched interests both inside and outside the education system that have little desire to shake things up to such a profound degree. As in the civil rights era, it may take the courts to compel the aggressive reforms needed to give all students a fair shot at a quality education. But thinking small while leaving dysfunctional educational structures intact absolutely guarantees that we will not accomplish the twin goals of educational excellence and equity. That much is clear.

Data Appendix

Here I briefly describe the series of projects that contributed to this book. I include relevant citations that provide more details on each of the indicated projects.

My first project in the curriculum space was funded by an anonymous foundation and had the goal of examining the alignment of mathematics textbooks to the Common Core State Standards. It specifically sought to test the common argument I had heard from teachers that publishers simply slapped an "aligned!" sticker on their pre–Common Core books. That project involved content analyzing seven popular elementary mathematics textbooks using the Surveys of Enacted Curriculum. The methods for that study are described in the *American Educational Research Journal*.[1]

Next, the National Science Foundation funded me to collect textbook adoption data in mathematics and science from the five most populous US states for the purposes of examining the feasibility of using these data to identify the impacts of various textbooks on student achievement. That project involved gathering administrative data from California districts' School Accountability Report Cards (SARCs) and sending Freedom of Information Act requests to every school district in New York, Texas, Florida, and Illinois. The methods for that study are described in *AERA Open* and also in a report published through the University of Southern California (USC) Center on Education Policy, Equity and Governance.[2]

A second study funded by an anonymous funder had two goals—to understand how districts make textbook adoption decisions and to estimate the student achievement effects of the most popular textbooks in California prior to the Common Core. We conducted semistructured interviews with district leaders representing thirty-four randomly selected districts across the state. We stratified districts on key characteristics we thought might be related to their adoption practices. The methods for that study are described in a recent paper published in the *Journal of Curriculum Studies*.[3] We also used the mathematics textbook adoption data from California schools' SARCs for the population of California elementary and middle schools in a statewide, quasi-experimental analysis of the impact of mathematics textbooks on student achievement. That research was published in *AERA Open*.[4]

I received two more grants—one from the William T. Grant Foundation and one from the Bill and Melinda Gates Foundation—to continue the SARC textbook data collection for an additional two years and augment it with other data sources. One project supported me to conduct interviews with eighth-grade mathematics teachers in the same thirty-four districts to understand their curriculum use and standards implementation. We compiled a list of eligible teachers in each district and randomly chose teachers to participate, aiming for three teachers per district. We ended up interviewing approximately sixty teachers. The other project had me as part of a large team collecting SARC textbook adoption data from multiple states to conduct a multistate impact study. These two projects contributed to a student's dissertation, to an ongoing research paper investigating inequality in students' opportunity to learn, to a large study of the effects of mathematics textbooks post–Common Core, and directly to this book.[5]

Recently, I was part of a multi-institution research center funded by the federal Institute of Education Sciences to study the implementation of college- and career-ready standards across the nation and in five partner states. There were many data collection activities in this project, but the most relevant to this work was a four-state deep-dive embedded multiple case study of school districts that we chose because they varied in size, demographics, and reform engagement. Data collection included classroom observations and interviews with teachers, coaches, and school and district leaders. The methods for this work are described in detail in *AERA Open*.[6]

Finally, I have recently been a part of a multistate study of the coherence of ELA teachers' instructional contexts and their instruction itself. We have partnered with Louisiana, Massachusetts, and Rhode Island to conduct interviews of state leaders and state-representative surveys of teachers and district leaders focused on these issues. The methods for this work are described in detail in a recent RAND report.[7]

I thank the funders for their generous support of my work over the last eight years. All opinions are mine; all errors are my own.

NOTES

CHAPTER 1

1. Marshall S. Smith and Jennifer O'Day, "Systemic School Reform," *Journal of Education Policy* 5, no. 5 (1990): 233–67. You can also see an update of their argument in their recent book *Opportunity for All*. Jennifer A. O'Day and Marshall S. Smith, *Opportunity for All: A Framework for Quality and Equality in Education* (Cambridge, MA: Harvard Education Press, 2019).
2. David P. Gardner et al., *A Nation at Risk: The Imperative for Educational Reform* (Washington, DC: National Commission on Excellence in Education, 1983).
3. Ibid., 1.
4. See, for instance, the early standards reforms in Texas and North Carolina. David Grissmer and Ann Flanagan, *Exploring Rapid Achievement Gains in North Carolina and Texas* (Washington, DC: National Education Goals Panel, 1998).
5. This section is a summary of Smith and O'Day, "Systemic School Reform."
6. P. David Pearson, "The Reading Wars," *Educational Policy* 18, no. 1 (2004): 216–52; Alan H. Schoenfeld, "The Math Wars," *Educational Policy* 18, no. 1 (2004): 253–86.
7. For a discussion of teacher control, see Richard M. Ingersoll, *Who Controls Teachers' Work? Power and Accountability in America's Schools* (Cambridge, MA: Harvard University Press, 2006).
8. This section, like the previous one, is mostly a summary of Smith and O'Day, "Systemic School Reform."
9. For instance, the federal Improving America's Schools Act of 1994, which reauthorized the Elementary and Secondary Education Act of 1965, did not require grade-level standards and required only grade-band assessment.
10. NCLB was the first federal law to require standards and assessments at each grade (standards for grades K–12, assessments each year in grades 3–8 and once in high school).
11. Gardner et al., *A Nation at Risk*.
12. Smith and O'Day, "Systemic School Reform," 239.

13. Jeannie Oakes, "Keeping Track, Part 1: The Policy and Practice of Curriculum Inequality," *Phi Delta Kappan* 68, no. 1 (1986): 12–17.
14. Dominic J. Brewer and Joanna Smith, *Evaluating the "Crazy Quilt": Educational Governance in California* (Los Angeles, CA: University of Southern California, 2006).
15. Fred M. Newmann, "Depth or Coverage in the School Curriculum?," *The Education Digest* 53, no. 9 (1988): 8.
16. James R. Flanders, "How Much of the Content in Mathematics Textbooks is New?," *Arithmetic Teacher* 35, no. 1 (1987): 18–23.
17. Judith W. Little, "District Policy Choices and Teachers' Professional Development Opportunities," *Educational Evaluation and Policy Analysis* 11, no. 2 (1989): 165–79.
18. Linda Darling-Hammond and Milbrey W. McLaughlin, "Policies That Support Professional Development in an Era of Reform," *Phi Delta Kappan* 76, no. 8 (1995): 597–604.
19. Thomas R. Guskey, "Professional Development in Education: In Search of the Optimal Mix" (paper presented at the annual meeting of the American Educational Research Association, New Orleans, Louisiana, April 4–8, 1994).
20. Morgan Polikoff, "The Challenges of Curriculum Materials as a Reform Lever," *Brookings Evidence Speaks Reports* 2, no. 58 (2018), https://www.brookings.edu/research/the-challenges-of-curriculum-materials-as-a-reform-lever/.
21. For overall impacts, see Thomas S. Dee and Brian Jacob, "The Impact of No Child Left Behind on Student Achievement," *Journal of Policy Analysis and Management* 30, no. 3 (2011): 418–446. For an argument that these gains are illusory, see Jennifer L. Jennings and Douglas Lee Lauen, "Accountability, Inequality, and Achievement: The Effects of the No Child Left Behind Act on Multiple Measures of Student Learning," *RSF: The Russell Sage Foundation Journal of the Social Sciences* 2, no. 5 (2016): 220–41.
22. Morgan S. Polikoff, "How Well Aligned Are Textbooks to the Common Core Standards in Mathematics?," *American Educational Research Journal* 52, no. 6 (2015): 1185–1211.
23. Cory Koedel et al., "Mathematics Curriculum Effects on Student Achievement in California," *AERA Open* 3, no. 1 (2017): 1–22; see also Morgan S. Polikoff et al., *Curriculum Counts: Math and Science Textbook Adoptions and Effects* (Los Angeles, CA: USC Rossier School of Education Center on Education Policy, Equity and Governance, 2020).
24. Morgan S. Polikoff et al., "The Formalized Processes Districts Use to Evaluate Mathematics Textbooks," *Journal of Curriculum Studies* 52, no. 4 (2019), 451–77.
25. Katie Pak et al., "The Adaptive Challenges of Curriculum Implementation: Insights for Educational Leaders Driving Standards-Based Reforms," *AERA Open* 6, no. 2 (2020), 1–15.
26. David Blazar et al., "Curriculum Reform in the Common Core Era: Evaluating Textbooks Using Student Achievement Data," *Journal of Policy Analysis and Management* 39, no. 4 (2020): 966–1019; Morgan Polikoff et al., *Exploring Coherence in ELA Instructional Systems in the Common Core Era* (Santa Monica, CA: RAND, 2020).

27. David K. Cohen, Stephen W. Raudenbush, and Deborah Loewenberg Ball, "Resources, Instruction, and Research," *Educational Evaluation and Policy Analysis* 25, no. 2 (2003): 119–42.

28. On pedagogical quality, see, for instance, Thomas Kane, Kerri Kerr, and Robert Pianta, *Designing Teacher Evaluation Systems: New Guidance from the Measures of Effective Teaching Project* (New York, NY: John Wiley & Sons, 2014). On curriculum, see, for instance, Polikoff, "The Challenges of Curriculum Materials."

CHAPTER 2

1. For a more complete discussion of these measurement issues, see Morgan S. Polikoff, "Instructional Alignment Under No Child Left Behind," *American Journal of Education* 118, no. 3 (2012): 341–68.

2. Brian M. Stecher and Sheila I. Barron, "Unintended Consequences of Test-Based Accountability When Testing in 'Milepost' Grades," *Educational Assessment* 7, no. 4 (2001): 259–81; Daniel M. Koretz et al., *Final Report: Perceived Effects of the Maryland School Performance Assessment Program* (Los Angeles, CA: National Center for Research on Evaluation, Standards, and Student Testing, 1996).

3. Mary L. Smith, *Reforming Schools by Reforming Assessment: Consequences of the Arizona Student Assessment Program (ASAP): Equity and Teacher Capacity-Building* (Los Angeles, CA: National Center for Research on Evaluation, Standards, and Student Testing, 1997.)

4. Lorraine M. McDonnell, *Politics, Persuasion, and Educational Testing* (Cambridge, MA: Harvard University Press, 2004).

5. For a more extended discussion of these validity issues, see Polikoff, "Instructional Alignment."

6. Ibid.

7. Ibid.

8. Morgan S. Polikoff, "Teacher Education, Experience, and the Practice of Aligned Instruction," *Journal of Teacher Education* 64, no. 3 (2013): 212–25.

9. John P. Papay and Matthew A. Kraft, "Productivity Returns to Experience in the Teacher Labor Market: Methodological Challenges and New Evidence on Long-Term Career Improvement," *Journal of Public Economics* 130 (2015): 105–119.

10. Morgan S. Polikoff, "The Association of State Policy Attributes with Teachers' Instructional Alignment," *Educational Evaluation and Policy Analysis* 34, no. 3 (2012): 278–94.

11. Heather C. Hill, "Policy Is Not Enough: Language and the Interpretation of State Standards," *American Educational Research Journal* 38, no. 2 (2001): 289–318.

12. James P. Spillane, *Standards Deviation: How Schools Misunderstand Education Policy* (Cambridge, MA: Harvard University Press, 2009).

13. Julia H. Kaufman et al., *Changes in What Teachers Know and Do in the Common Core Era: American Teacher Panel Findings from 2015 to 2017* (Santa Monica, CA: RAND, 2018).

14. For more on this issue, see Morgan S. Polikoff, "Is Common Core Working? And Where Does Common Core Research Go from Here? Introduction to the Special Topic on Implementation and Preliminary Effects of the Common Core Standards," *AERA Open*, 3, no. 1 (2017): 1–6.

15. Thomas S. Dee and Brian Jacob, "The Impact of No Child Left Behind on Student Achievement," *Journal of Policy Analysis and Management* 30, no. 3 (2011): 418–46; Manyee Wong et al., "Adding Design Elements to Improve Time Series Designs: No Child Left Behind as an Example of Causal Pattern-matching," *Journal of Research on Educational Effectiveness* 8, no. 2 (2015): 245–79.

16. Dee and Jacob, "The Impact of No Child Left Behind."

17. Fourth-grade math is shown for conciseness, but the patterns of gap closing are not markedly different in other subjects and grades.

18. Dee and Jacob, "The Impact of No Child Left Behind."

19. S. Michael Gaddis and Douglas L. Lauen, "School Accountability and the Black–White Test Score Gap," *Social Science Research* 44 (2014): 15–31; Douglas L. Lauen and S. Michael Gaddis, "Shining a Light or Fumbling in the Dark? The Effects of NCLB's Subgroup-Specific Accountability on Student Achievement," *Educational Evaluation and Policy Analysis* 34, no. 2 (2012): 185–208.

20. Of course, any study conducted in any public school setting in the last two decades is in some sense in the context of standards-based reforms. These turnaround studies all took place in states that had all the core elements of standards-based reform, but the studies are about the impact of accountability (in this case, in the form of turn-around policies) on outcomes, holding constant standards-related policies.

21. See, for instance, Atila Abdulkadiroğlu et al., "Charters Without Lotteries: Testing Takeovers in New Orleans and Boston," *American Economic Review* 106, no. 7 (2016): 1878–920; Beth E. Schueler, Joshua S. Goodman, and David J. Deming, "Can States Take Over and Turn Around School Districts? Evidence from Lawrence, Massachusetts," *Educational Evaluation and Policy Analysis* 39, no. 2 (2017): 311–32; Ron Zimmer, Gary T. Henry, and Adam Kho, "The Effects of School Turnaround in Tennessee's Achievement School District and Innovation Zones," *Educational Evaluation and Policy Analysis* 39, no. 4 (2017): 670–96.

22. Helen F. Ladd, "The Dallas School Accountability and Incentive Program: An Evaluation of Its Impacts on Student Outcomes," *Economics of Education Review* 18, no. 1 (1999): 1–16.

23. Mengli Song, Rui Yang, and Michael Garet, *Effects of States' Implementation of College- and Career-Ready Standards on Student Achievement* (Philadelphia, PA: Center on Standards, Alignment, Instruction, and Learning, 2019).

24. It may be that the alignment of NAEP to new standards has something to do with this finding. As mentioned earlier in the chapter, it is not at all obvious how to choose an outcome measure to evaluate the impact of standards.

25. Linda Darling-Hammond, "Evaluating 'No Child Left Behind,'" *The Nation* 284, no. 20 (2007): 11.

26. Jennifer L. Jennings and Jonathan M. Bearak, "'Teaching to the Test' in the NCLB Era: How Test Predictability Affects Our Understanding of Student Performance," *Educational Researcher* 43, no. 8 (2014): 381–89; Morgan S. Polikoff, Andrew C. Porter, and John Smithson, "How Well Aligned Are State Assessments of Student Achievement with State Content Standards?," *American Educational Research Journal* 48, no. 4 (2011): 965–95.

27. Polikoff, Porter, and Smithson, "How Well Aligned."

28. Jennings and Bearak, "Teaching to the Test"; see also Rebecca Holcombe, Jennifer Jennings, and Daniel Koretz, "The Roots of Score Inflation: An Examination of Opportunities in Two States' Tests," in *Charting Reform, Achieving Equity in a Diverse Nation*, ed. Gail L. Sunderman (Greenwich, CT: Information Age Publishing, 2013).

29. Nancy Doorey and Morgan Polikoff, *Evaluating the Content and Quality of Next Generation Assessments* (Washington, DC: Thomas B. Fordham Institute, 2016).

30. Koretz et. al, *Final Report: Perceived Effects.*

31. Catherine Gewertz, "New Setback for PARCC as Another State Abandons Test," *Education Week* 38, no. 18 (2019): 10.

32. There are many critiques of NCLB-era and post-NCLB accountability systems. For NCLB-era systems, see, for instance, Robert L. Linn, Eva L. Baker, and Damian W. Betebenner, "Accountability Systems: Implications of Requirements of the No Child Left Behind Act of 2001," *Educational Researcher* 31, no. 6 (2002): 3–16; Andrew C. Porter, Robert L. Linn, and C. Scott Trimble, "The Effects of State Decisions About NCLB Adequate Yearly Progress Targets," *Educational Measurement: Issues and Practice* 24, no. 4 (2005): 32–39. For post-NCLB systems, see Andrew McEachin and Morgan S. Polikoff, "We Are the 5%: Which Schools Would Be Held Accountable Under a Proposed Revision of the Elementary and Secondary Education Act?" *Educational Researcher* 41, no. 7 (2012): 243–51; Morgan S. Polikoff et al., "The Waive of the Future? School Accountability in the Waiver Era, *Educational Researcher* 43, no. 1 (2014): 45–54.

33. Heather Vogell, "Investigation into APS Cheating Finds Unethical Behavior Across Every Level," *Atlanta Journal-Constitution*, Aug 23, 2019, https://www.ajc.com/news/local/investigation-into-aps-cheating-finds-unethical-behavior-across-every-level/bX4bEZDWbeOH33cDkod1FL/.

34. Linn, Baker, and Betebenner, "Accountability Systems: Implications."

35. Polikoff et al., "The Waive of the Future."

36. Chad Aldeman et al., *An Independent Review of ESSA State Plans* (Washington, DC: Bellwether Education Partners, 2017).

37. Phi Delta Kappan, *Frustration in the Schools* (Washington, DC: Phi Delta Kappan, 2019).

38. Sheila B. Carmichael et al., *The State of State Standards—and the Common Core—in 2010* (Washington, DC: Thomas B. Fordham Institute, 2010).

39. Andrew C. Porter, Morgan S. Polikoff, and John Smithson, "Is There a De Facto National Intended Curriculum? Evidence from State Content Standards," *Educational Evaluation and Policy Analysis* 31, no. 3 (2009): 238–68.

40. For concerns about the age appropriateness of the ELA standards, for example, see Laura F. Main, "Too Much Too Soon? Common Core Math Standards in the Early Years," *Early Childhood Education Journal* 40, no. 2 (2012): 73–77. For concerns about the content of the mathematics standards, for example, see Ze'ev Wurman and W. Stephen Wilson, "The Common Core Math Standards: Are They a Step Forward or Backward?" *Education Next* 12, no. 3 (2012): 45–50.

41. William H. Schmidt, Curtis C. McKnight, and Senta A. Raizen, *A Splintered Vision: An Investigation of U.S. Science and Mathematics Education* (Dordrecht, NL: Springer, 1997).

42. Morgan S. Polikoff, "How Well Aligned Are Textbooks to the Common Core Standards in Mathematics?," *American Educational Research Journal* 52, no. 6 (2015): 1185–211; William H. Schmidt and Richard T. Houang, "US Mathematics Textbooks in the Common Core Era: A First Look," in *Proceedings of the International Conferences on Mathematics Textbook Research and Development*, ed. Keith Jones et al. (Southampton, UK: University of Southampton, 2014).

43. Kaufman et al., *Changes in What Teachers Know.*

44. Julia H. Kaufman, Lindsey E. Thompson, and V. Darleen Opfer, *Creating a Coherent System to Support Instruction Aligned with State Standards: Promising Practices of the Louisiana Department of Education* (Santa Monica, CA: RAND, 2016).

45. Laura M. Desimone, "Improving Impact Studies of Teachers' Professional Development: Toward Better Conceptualizations and Measures," *Educational Researcher* 38, no. 3 (2009): 181–99.

46. David Blazar et al., *Learning by the Book: Comparing Math Achievement Growth by Textbook in Six Common Core States* (Cambridge, MA: Center for Education Policy Research, Harvard University, 2019).

47. Cory Koedel et al., "Teacher Preparation Programs and Teacher Quality: Are There Real Differences Across Programs?" *Education Finance and Policy* 10, no. 4 (2015): 508–34.

48. National Council on Teacher Quality, *2018 Teacher Prep Review* (Washington, DC: National Council on Teacher Quality, 2018).

CHAPTER 3

1. For some groundbreaking recent work on this topic, visit www.EdBuild.org or see their recent reports on the role of school districts in perpetuating socioeconomic and racial inequality. See also National Academies of Sciences, Engineering, & Medicine, *Monitoring Educational Equity* (Washington, DC: National Academies Press, 2019).

2. See Morgan Polikoff, "The Challenges of Curriculum Materials as a Reform Lever," *Brookings Evidence Speaks Reports* 2, no. 58 (2018): 1–11; see also Morgan S. Polikoff et al., *Curriculum Counts: Math and Science Textbook Adoptions and Effects* (Los Angeles, CA: USC Rossier School of Education Center on Education Policy, Equity and Governance, 2020).

3. Marshall S. Smith and Jennifer O'Day, "Systemic School Reform," *Journal of Education Policy* 5, no. 5 (1990): 233–67.

4. I sometimes use the word "standardization," especially when I am referring to negative arguments that are made against standards-based instructional reforms. Other

times I use the words "consistency," "coherence," or "alignment," which are closely related but less polarizing terms.

5. Michelle R. Davis, "'Big Three' Publishers Rethink K–12 Strategies," *Education Week* 6, no. 2 (2013): 42–44.

6. For more on this issue, see Polikoff, "The Challenges of Curriculum Materials."

7. David Blazar et al., *Learning by the Book: Comparing Math Achievement Growth by Textbook in Six Common Core States* (Cambridge, MA: Center for Education Policy Research, Harvard University, 2019).

8. Morgan Polikoff et al., *Exploring Coherence in ELA Instructional Systems in the Common Core Era* (Santa Monica, CA: RAND, 2020).

9. Ibid.

10. See edreports.org for all of the available reviews.

11. Morgan S. Polikoff, "How Well Aligned Are Textbooks to the Common Core Standards in Mathematics?," *American Educational Research Journal* 52, no. 6 (2015): 1185–211.

12. This work is not yet published, but these data are available from the author upon request.

13. https://www.engageny.org/resource/grade-6-mathematics-module-2-topic-b-lesson-9.

14. https://access.openupresources.org/curricula/our6-8math/en/grade-6/unit-5/lesson-3/index.html.

15. http://www.corestandards.org/Math/Content/introduction/how-to-read-the-grade-level-standards/.

16. See edreports.org and Polikoff, "How Well Aligned Are Textbooks?"

17. William H. Schmidt et al., *Why Schools Matter: A Cross-National Comparison of Curriculum and Learning* (San Francisco, CA: Jossey-Bass, 2001).

18. Davis, "'Big Three' Publishers."

19. Of course, there are other states that collect these data now or have in the past—not many, but not zero—suggesting that it can be possible to collect textbook data without usurping local control over textbook decisions.

20. Catherine Gewertz, "States Ceding Power Over Classroom Materials," *Education Week* 34, no. 21 (2015): 1.

21. See details about California's adoption process at http://www.cde.ca.gov/ci/ma/im/.

22. See, for instance, Mike Bowler, "Textbook Publishers Try to Please All, but First They Woo the Heart of Texas," *The Reading Teacher* 31, no. 5 (1978): 514–18; Raymond English, "The Politics of Textbook Adoption," *The Phi Delta Kappan* 62, no. 4 (1980): 275–78; Chester E. Finn and Diane Ravitch, *The Mad, Mad World of Textbook Adoption* (Washington, DC: Thomas B. Fordham Institute, 2004).

23. Finn and Ravitch, *The Mad, Mad World*.

24. Louisiana is also an excellent example because it shows that control over curriculum in public schools need not imply the death of pluralism. The state has a widely studied (and not very effective) voucher program that sends thousands of children to private schools. See, for instance, Jonathan N. Mills and Patrick J. Wolf, "Vouchers in the Bayou: The Effects of the Louisiana Scholarship Program on Student Achievement After 2 Years," *Educational Evaluation and Policy Analysis* 39, no. 3 (2017): 464–84.

25. Julia H. Kaufman, Lindsey E. Thompson, and V. Darleen Opfer, *Creating a Coherent System to Support Instruction Aligned with State Standards: Promising Practices of the Louisiana Department of Education* (Santa Monica, CA: RAND, 2016).

26. See louisianabelieves.com for all available ratings.

27. Polikoff et al., *Exploring Coherence.*

28. Kaufman et al., *Creating a Coherent System,* 16.

29. Chiefs for Change, *Leading Change in Louisiana: How Louisiana is Empowering Teachers to Implement an Aligned Academic Vision* (Washington, DC: Chiefs for Change, 2020).

30. Morgan S. Polikoff et al., "The Formalized Processes Districts Use to Evaluate Mathematics Textbooks," *Journal of Curriculum Studies* 52, no. 4 (2020): 451–77.

CHAPTER 4

1. Dan C. Lortie, *Schoolteacher: A Sociological Study* (Chicago, IL: University of Chicago Press, 1975).

2. See, for instance, Susan M. Johnson, "Will VAMS Reinforce the Walls of the Egg-Crate School?" *Educational Researcher* 44, no. 2 (2015): 117–26.

3. Though it is not clear that incentive pay programs affect teacher motivation or instruction; see Kun Yuan et al., "Incentive Pay Programs Do Not Affect Teacher Motivation or Reported Practices: Results From Three Randomized Studies," *Educational Evaluation and Policy Analysis* 35, no. 1 (2013): 3–22.

4. Educators for Excellence, *Voices from the Classroom: A Survey of America's Educators* (New York: Educators for Excellence, 2018); see also Elizabeth Green, *Building a Better Teacher: How Teaching Works (and How to Teach It to Everyone)* (New York: W.W. Norton & Company, 2010).

5. Lortie, *Schoolteacher.* For a review of who becomes a teacher, see also Cassandra M. Guarino, Lucrecia Santibañez, and Glenn A. Daley, "Teacher Recruitment and Retention: A Review of the Recent Empirical Literature," *Review of Educational Research* 76, no. 2 (2006): 173–208.

6. Guarino, Santibañez, and Daley, "Teacher Recruitment."

7. Matthew A. Kraft and Allison F. Gilmour, "Revisiting *The Widget Effect*: Teacher Evaluation Reforms and the Distribution of Teacher Effectiveness," *Educational Researcher* 46, no. 5 (2017): 234–49; see also Green, *Building a Better Teacher.*

8. Morgan Polikoff et al., *Exploring Coherence in ELA Instructional Systems in the Common Core Era* (Santa Monica, CA: RAND, 2020).

9. Richard M. Ingersoll, *Who Controls Teachers' Work? Power and Accountability in America's Schools* (Cambridge, MA: Harvard University Press, 2003).

10. Jason A. Grissom, Sean Nicholson-Crotty, and James R. Harrington, "Estimating the Effects of No Child Left Behind on Teachers' Work Environments and Job Attitudes," *Educational Evaluation and Policy Analysis* 36, no. 4 (2014): 417–36.

11. In recent work, my PhD student Dan Silver and I argue that "supplementation" is undertheorized, and indeed that supplementation can mean many different kinds of behaviors. Here, I take supplementation to refer to using materials other than the main

instructional materials that are formally adopted by the school or district. This is distinct from, but related to, modification, where teachers use the main materials but change them in certain ways during implementation.

12. Katie Tosh et al., *Digital Instructional Materials: What Are Teachers Using and What Barriers Exist?* (Santa Monica, CA: RAND, 2020).

13. V. D. Opfer, Julia H. Kaufman, and Lindsey E. Thompson, *Implementation of K–12 State Standards for Mathematics and English Language Arts and Literacy* (Santa Monica, CA: RAND, 2016).

14. By teacher-created materials, I mean those obtained from online lesson repositories, materials they created themselves, materials created by colleagues at their school, or materials in their personal library but not provided by their school. See also Polikoff et al., *Exploring Coherence*.

15. Morgan Polikoff and Jennifer Dean, *The Supplemental Curriculum Bazaar: Is What's Online Any Good?* (Washington, DC: Thomas B. Fordham Institute, 2019).

16. Polikoff and Dean, *The Supplemental Curriculum Bazaar*.

17. Whether tight curriculum control—or something approaching a truly scripted curriculum—is a good thing is a thorny and highly contentious question. Certainly most teacher educators are highly resistant to scripted curricula (just search for "scripted curriculum" on Google Scholar if you want proof of this claim), and there is reason to be concerned about the equity implications of scripted curricula (see, e.g., H. R. Milner IV, "Scripted and Narrowed Curriculum Reform in Urban Schools," *Urban Education* 48, no. 2 [2013], 163–70). But there are also some scripted curricula that have shown impressive achievement effects for students (see, e.g., Robert E. Slavin et al., *Two Million Children: Success for All* (Thousand Oaks, CA: Corwin, 2009), and some evidence suggests that scripts can be educative for teachers (see, e.g., Janine Remillard and Luke Reinke, "Complicating Scripted Curriculum: Can Scripts Be Educative for Teachers?" [paper presented at the annual meeting of the American Educational Research Association, Vancouver, BC, April 13–17, 2012).

18. For a recent review of alignment methods, see Morgan Polikoff, "Alignment," in *Routledge Encyclopedia of Education*, ed. S. Brookhart, forthcoming.

19. This work was supported by grants from the Smith Richardson and the William T. Grant Foundations.

20. Polikoff and Dean, *The Supplemental Curriculum Bazaar*, 32.

21. David Blazar et al., *Learning by the Book: Comparing Math Achievement Growth by Textbook in Six Common Core States* (Cambridge, MA: Center for Education Policy Research, Harvard University, 2019).

22. Opfer, Kaufman, and Thompson, *Implementation of K–12 State Standards*.

23. Marci Goldberg, *Classroom Trends: Teachers as Buyers of Instructional Materials and Users of Technology* (Shelton, CT: MDR, 2016).

24. There is a cottage industry of these kinds of news stories. Consider the slavery role-playing game that was taught in a North Carolina elementary school or the lesson that told a largely Latino group of California elementary school students "You just CAN'T cross the border of the U.S." The Associated Press, "NC School's Slavery Role-Playing

Game Prompts Investigation," March 12, 2019, https://apnews.com/article/1b97a219 81564df5acf9d87fb7c8b35d; Erick Galindo, "How Angry Parents Annihilated a 'Racist' Study Guide Given to Their Downey 5th Graders," *LAist*, November 22, 2019, https://laist.com/2019/11/22/racist_study_guide_map_handout_downey_5th_graders _parents_battle.php.

25. There were a few modest differences in modification frequency; for instance, 38 percent of Louisiana teachers said they modified materials at least once a week because the materials were too challenging, versus 45 percent of Rhode Island teachers and 52 percent of Massachusetts teachers.

26. Polikoff and Dean, *The Supplemental Curriculum Bazaar.*

27. Shauna Campbell, "Disruptions to the Traditional Textbook Narrative: Lessons from District Leaders and Teachers in California" (PhD diss., University of Southern California, 2019).

28. Emma García, "It's the Beginning of the School Year and Teachers Are Once Again Opening Up Their Wallets to Buy School Supplies," *Working Economics Blog*, August 22, 2019, https://www.epi.org/blog/teachers-are-buying-school-supplies/.

29. Polikoff et al., *Exploring Coherence.*

CHAPTER 5

1. This is an elaboration of some data presented in chapter 2. See Julia H. Kaufman et al., *Changes in What Teachers Know and Do in the Common Core Era: American Teacher Panel Findings from 2015 to 2017* (Santa Monica, CA: RAND Corporation, 2018).

2. The survey also asked teachers to order a set of standards from low to high grade level and to identify the "aspects of rigor" in a set of standards. On these two tests, about one-quarter and one-half of teachers, respectively, got the question correct.

3. http://www.corestandards.org/about-the-standards/myths-vs-facts/.

4. Heather C. Hill, "Policy Is Not Enough: Language and the Interpretation of State Standards," *American Educational Research Journal* 38, no. 2 (2001): 289–318.

5. James P. Spillane, *Standards Deviation: How Schools Misunderstand Education Policy* (Cambridge, MA: Harvard University Press, 2006).

6. Hill, "Policy Is Not Enough."

7. http://www.corestandards.org/Math/Practice/.

8. Michael Fullan and Joanne Quinn, *Coherence: The Right Drivers in Action for Schools, Districts, and Systems* (Thousand Oaks, CA: Corwin Press, 2016).

9. Morgan Polikoff et al., *Exploring Coherence in ELA Instructional Systems in the Common Core Era* (Santa Monica, CA: RAND, 2020).

10. Of course, we cannot know whether teachers' self-created materials are well aligned with standards. However, given the results reported earlier about teachers' understanding of the standards it seems unlikely that these materials are, on average, standards aligned.

11. Michael S. Garet et al., "What Makes Professional Development Effective? Results

from a National Sample of Teachers," *American Educational Research Journal* 38, no. 4 (2001): 915–45.

12. As a reminder, the four policy supports are receiving at least four of seven possible curriculum-related supports, receiving at least one multiday curriculum-related professional development activity, having interim assessments at least moderately aligned with other instructional supports, and having evaluations focused on instructional alignment and supporting diverse students to at least a moderate extent.

13. Julia H. Kaufman, Lindsey E. Thompson, and V. Darleen Opfer, *Creating a Coherent System to Support Instruction Aligned with State Standards: Promising Practices of the Louisiana Department of Education* (Santa Monica, CA: RAND, 2016).

14. Polikoff et al., *Exploring Coherence.*

15. David Blazar et al., *Learning by the Book: Comparing Math Achievement Growth by Textbook in Six Common Core States* (Cambridge, MA: Center for Education Policy Research, Harvard University, 2019).

16. Michael S. Garet et al., "What Makes Professional Development Effective? Results From a National Sample of Teachers," *American Educational Research Journal* 38, no. 4 (2001): 915–45; see also Laura M. Desimone, "Improving Impact Studies of Teachers' Professional Development: Toward Better Conceptualizations and Measures," *Educational Researcher* 38, no. 3 (2009): 181–99.

17. Portions of this section are based on the dissertation research of one of my PhD advisees, Shauna Campbell. Shauna Campbell, "Disruptions to the Traditional Textbook Narrative: Lessons from District Leaders and Teachers in California" (PhD diss., University of Southern California, 2019).

18. Ronald A. Heifetz, Alexander Grashow, and Marty Linsky, *The Practice of Adaptive Leadership: Tools and Tactics for Changing Your Organization and the World* (Cambridge, MA: Harvard Business Press, 2009).

19. Katie Pak et al., "The Adaptive Challenges of Curriculum Implementation: Insights for Educational Leaders Driving Standards-Based Reforms," *AERA Open* 6, no. 2 (2020), 1–15.

CHAPTER 6

1. OECD, *Education at a Glance 2019* (Paris: OECD Publishing, 2019).

2. Ibid.

3. Dorothea Anagnostopoulos, "Testing and Student Engagement with Literature in Urban Classrooms: A Multi-Layered Perspective," *Research in the Teaching of English* (2003): 177–212; Morgan S. Polikoff and Kathryn Struthers, "Changes in the Cognitive Complexity of English Instruction: The Moderating Effects of School and Classroom Characteristics," *Teachers College Record* 115, no. 8 (2013): 1–26; Linda Valli and Marilyn Chambliss, "Creating Classroom Cultures: One Teacher, Two Lessons, and a High-Stakes Test," *Anthropology & Education Quarterly* 38, no. 1 (2007): 57–75.

4. Rebecca M. Callahan, "Tracking and High School English Learners: Limiting

Opportunity to Learn," *American Educational Research Journal* 42, no. 2 (2005): 305–28; Alexander Kurz et al., "Assessing Opportunity-to-Learn for Students with Disabilities in General and Special Education Classes," *Assessment for Effective Intervention* 40, no. 1 (2014): 24–39.

5. Julia H. Kaufman, Lindsey E. Thompson, and V. Darleen Opfer, *Creating a Coherent System to Support Instruction Aligned with State Standards: Promising Practices of the Louisiana Department of Education* (Santa Monica, CA: RAND, 2016).

6. Dan Goldhaber, John M. Krieg, and Roddy Theobald, "Does the Match Matter? Exploring Whether Student Teaching Experiences Affect Teacher Effectiveness," *American Educational Research Journal* 54, no. 2 (2017): 325–59; Matthew Ronfeldt et al., "Identifying Promising Clinical Placements Using Administrative Data: Preliminary Results from ISTI Placement Initiative Pilot" (CALDER working paper 189, CALDER, Washington, DC, 2018).

7. Margaret E. Goertz, Leslie Nabors Oláh, and Matthew Riggan, *From Testing to Teaching: The Use of Interim Assessments in Classroom Instruction* (Philadelphia, PA: Consortium for Policy Research in Education, 2009).

8. Roberto Agodini et al., *Achievement Effects of Four Early Elementary School Math Curricula: Findings for First and Second Graders. NCEE 2011–4001* (Washington, DC: National Center for Education Evaluation and Regional Assistance, 2010); Rachana Bhatt and Cory Koedel, "Large-Scale Evaluations of Curricular Effectiveness: The Case of Elementary Mathematics in Indiana," *Educational Evaluation and Policy Analysis* 34, no. 4 (2012): 391–412; Rachana Bhatt, Cory Koedel, and Douglas Lehmann, "Is Curriculum Quality Uniform? Evidence from Florida," *Economics of Education Review* 34 (2013): 107–21; Cory Koedel et al., "Mathematics Curriculum Effects on Student Achievement in California," *AERA Open* 3, no. 1 (2017): 1–22.

9. Koedel et al., "Mathematics Curriculum Effects."

10. David Blazar et al., *Learning by the Book: Comparing Math Achievement Growth by Textbook in Six Common Core States* (Cambridge, MA: Center for Education Policy Research, Harvard University, 2019).

11. See https://www.c-sail.org/ for a full description of the broader project.

12. Katie Pak et al., "The Adaptive Challenges of Curriculum Implementation: Insights for Educational Leaders Driving Standards-Based Reforms," *AERA Open* 6, no. 2 (2020), 1–15.

13. Ann Podolsky et al., *California's Positive Outliers: Districts Beating the Odds* (Palo Alto, CA: Learning Policy Institute, 2019).

14. Innovate Public Schools, *2020 Top Los Angeles County Public Schools* (Los Angeles, CA: Innovate Public Schools, 2020).

15. The other two principles of effective professional learning are content focus and coherence, but these are automatic in professional learning focused on the adopted materials. See Laura M. Desimone, "Improving Impact Studies of Teachers' Professional Development: Toward Better Conceptualizations and Measures," *Educational Researcher* 38, no. 3 (2009): 181–99.

16. Blazar et al., *Learning by the Book.*
17. Ibid.
18. Morgan Polikoff and Jennifer Dean, *The Supplemental Curriculum Bazaar: Is What's Online Any Good?* (Washington, DC: Thomas B. Fordham Institute, 2019).
19. Morgan S. Polikoff et al., "The Formalized Processes Districts Use to Evaluate Mathematics Textbooks," *Journal of Curriculum Studies* 52, no. 4 (2019): 451–77.
20. Wayne A. Welch, "Twenty Years of Science Curriculum Development: A Look Back," *Review of Research in Education* 7 (1979): 282–306.
21. Welch, "Twenty Years of Science Curriculum"; see also Stanley L. Helgeson, Patricia E. Blosser, and Robert W. Howe, *The Status of Pre-College Science, Mathematics, and Social Science Education: 1955–1975*, vol. I (Columbus, OH: Center for Science and Mathematics Education, The Ohio State University, 1977).
22. Helgeson et al., *The Status of Pre-College Science.*
23. Robert E. Yager, "Viewpoint: What We Did Not Learn from the 60s About Science Curriculum Reform," *Journal of Research in Science Teaching* 29, no. 8 (1992): 905–910.
24. The studies by Stanford's Center for Research on Education Outcomes (CREDO) generally find extremely modest differences between charters and traditional public schools in the same market. See, for instance, James L. Woodworth et al., *Charter Management Organizations* (Stanford, CA: Center for Research on Education Outcomes, 2017).
25. C. K. Jackson, Rucker C. Johnson, and Claudia Persico, "The Effects of School Spending on Educational Economic Outcomes: Evidence from School Finance Reforms," *The Quarterly Journal of Economics* 131, no. 1 (2016): 157–218; Christian Buerger, Seung Hyeong Lee, and John D. Singleton, *Test-Based Accountability and the Effectiveness of School Finance Reforms* (Providence, RI: Annenberg Institute at Brown University, 2020).
26. Ethan Hutt and Morgan S. Polikoff, "Toward a Framework for Public Accountability in Education Reform," *Educational Researcher* 49, no. 7 (2020): 503–511.
27. Of course, there are some exceptions to this, and some proportion of teachers will probably never use adopted core materials unless they are compelled to.
28. It is worth pointing out that teacher grade switching is extremely common—much more so than mobility in and out of the profession. About a sixth of teachers change grades each year. See David Blazar, "Grade Assignments and the Teacher Pipeline: A Low-Cost Lever to Improve Student Achievement," *Educational Research* 44, no. 4 (2015): 213–27.
29. Blazar et al., *Learning by the Book.*
30. Paula B. Baker and Lee W. Digiovanni, "Narratives on Culturally Relevant Pedagogy: Personal Responses to the Standardized Curriculum," *Current Issues in Education* 8, no. 22 (2005): 1–11.
31. Morgan Polikoff et al., *Exploring Coherence in ELA Instructional Systems in the Common Core Era* (Santa Monica, CA: RAND, 2020).

CHAPTER 7

1. Sally Chung, *Williams v. California: Lessons from Nine Years of Implementation* (Los Angeles: ACLU Foundation of Southern California, 2013).
2. Ibid., 11.
3. Ibid., 11.
4. Christopher Edley Jr. and Hayin Kimner, *Education Equity in California* (Stanford, CA: Policy Analysis for California Education, 2018).
5. Ethan Hutt and Morgan S. Polikoff, "Toward a Framework for Public Accountability in Education Reform," *Educational Researcher* 49, no. 7 (2020): 503–511; Ethan Hutt and Morgan Polikoff, "Reasonable Expectations: A Reply to Elmendorf and Shanshke," *University of Illinois Law Review Online* (Spring 2018): 194–208.
6. Jeannie Oakes, "Introduction to: Education Inadequacy, Inequality, and Failed State Policy: A Synthesis of Expert Reports Prepared for Williams v. State of California," *Santa Clara Law Review* 43 (2002): 1299–398.
7. Author's calculations from the National Assessment of Educational Progress Data Explorer, https://nces.ed.gov/nationsreportcard/data.
8. Morgan S. Polikoff et al., "The Formalized Processes Districts Use to Evaluate Mathematics Textbooks," *Journal of Curriculum Studies* 52, no. 4 (2019): 451–77.
9. Hutt and Polikoff, "Toward a Framework."
10. Morgan Polikoff, "The Challenges of Curriculum Materials as a Reform Lever," *Brookings Evidence Speaks Reports* 2, no. 58 (2018): 1–11.
11. Hutt and Polikoff, "Reasonable Expectations."
12. http://www.engageny.org.
13. Julia H. Kaufman et al., *Use of Open Educational Resources in an Era of Common Standards: A Case Study on the Use of EngageNY* (Santa Monica, CA: RAND Corporation, 2017).
14. I exclude generic materials like "leveled readers," which simply pair children with texts at their reading level, in these rankings.
15. Pub. L. No. 90-247, title IV, §438.
16. Morgan Polikoff et al., *Exploring Coherence in ELA Instructional Systems in the Common Core Era* (Santa Monica, CA: RAND, 2020).
17. Larry V. Hedges and Eric C. Hedberg, "Intraclass Correlation Values for Planning Group-Randomized Trials in Education," *Educational Evaluation and Policy Analysis* 29, no. 1 (2007): 60–87.
18. Dana Goldstein, "Detroit Students Have a Constitutional Right to Literacy, Court Rules," *New York Times*, April 28, 2020, A17.
19. For a recent example that cites other relevant studies showing positive effects, see Cory Koedel et al., "Mathematics Curriculum Effects on Student Achievement in California," *AERA Open* 3, no. 1 (2017): 1–22. For a counterexample, see David Blazar et al., *Learning by the Book: Comparing Math Achievement Growth by Textbook in Six Common Core States* (Cambridge, MA: Center for Education Policy Research, Harvard University, 2019).

20. Julia H. Kaufman, Lindsey E. Thompson, and V. Darleen Opfer, *Creating a Coherent System to Support Instruction Aligned with State Standards: Promising Practices of the Louisiana Department of Education* (Santa Monica, CA: RAND, 2016).

CHAPTER 8

1. Ashley Jochim, Bryan C. Hassel, and Beth Clifford, "States Must Take Decisive Action to Avert the Coming Education Crisis," *The Lens*, July 29, 2020, https://www.crpe.org /thelens/states-must-take-decisive-action-avert-coming-education-crisis.
2. Betheny Gross and Alice Opalka, "Too Many Schools Leave Learning to Chance During the Pandemic," *The Lens*, June 10, 2020, https://www.crpe.org/publications /too-many-schools-leave-learning-chance-during-pandemic.
3. Jon Valant, "School Reopening Plans Linked to Politics Rather Than Public Health," *Brown Center Chalkboard*, July 29, 2020, https://www.brookings.edu/blog/brown -center-chalkboard/2020/07/29/school-reopening-plans-linked-to-politics-rather -than-public-health/.
4. Mike Garet et al., *National Survey on Public Education's Coronavirus Pandemic Response* (Washington, DC: American Institutes for Research, 2020).
5. Morgan Polikoff, Anna R. Saavedra, and Shira Korn, "Not All Kids Have Computers—And They're Being Left Behind with Schools Closed by the Coronavirus," *The Conversation*, May 8, 2020, https://theconversation.com/not-all-kids-have -computers-and-theyre-being-left-behind-with-schools-closed-by-the-coronavirus -137359.
6. This discussion does not deal with the very real threat posed by elected officials at the state level and above who not only deny scientific truth but actively seek to thwart the use of science to inform decisions. That is a separate problem for a separate book—for a good discussion of what to do about that problem, see Gale M. Sinatra and Barbara K. Hofer, *Science Denial: Why It Happens and What to Do About It* (New York, NY: Oxford University Press, forthcoming).
7. For a recent discussion, see Paul Manna and Patrick McGuinn, *Education Governance for the Twenty-First Century: Overcoming the Structural Barriers to School Reform* (Washington, DC: Brookings Institution Press, 2013).
8. For a more comprehensive list of factors, see National Academies of Sciences, Engineering and Medicine, *Monitoring Educational Equity* (Washington, DC: National Academies Press, 2019).
9. For an excellent and even stronger critique of school districts, see Kevin Carey, "No More School Districts!" *Democracy*, no. 55 (2019), https://democracyjournal.org/ magazine/55/no-more-school-districts/.
10. Author's calculations from the Digest of Education Statistics. https://nces.ed.gov/ programs/digest/.
11. Author's calculations based on the Urban Institute Education Data Portal, https:// educationdata.urban.org/data-explorer/.
12. https://edbuild.org/content/dismissed.

13. https://edbuild.org/content/fractured.

14. https://edbuild.org/content/fault-lines.

15. Kendra Bischoff, "School District Fragmentation and Racial Residential Segregation," *Urban Affairs Review* 44, no. 2 (2008): 182–217.

16. https://edbuild.org/content/23-billion; see also Victoria E. Sosina and Ericka S. Weathers, "Pathways to Inequality: Between-District Segregation and Racial Disparities in School District Expenditures," *AERA Open* 5, no. 3 (2019): 1–15.

17. Sandra E. Black and Stephen Machin, "Housing Valuations of School Performance," *Handbook of the Economics of Education* 3 (2011): 485–519.

18. Donald Boyd et al., "The Draw of Home: How Teachers' Preferences for Proximity Disadvantage Urban Schools," *Journal of Policy Analysis and Management* 24 (2005): 113–32; see also Hamilton Lankford, Susanna Loeb, and James Wyckoff, "Teacher Sorting and the Plight of Urban Schools: A Descriptive Analysis," *Educational Evaluation and Policy Analysis* 24 (2002): 37–62.

19. For a recent discussion of the literature on democratic engagement, see Ethan Hutt and Morgan S. Polikoff, "Toward a Framework for Public Accountability in Education Reform, *Educational Researcher* 49, no. 7 (2020): 503–511.

20. Frederick M. Hess and Olivia Meeks, *School Boards Circa 2010: Governance in the Accountability Era* (Washington, DC: The National School Boards Association, The Thomas B. Fordham Institute, and the Iowa School Boards Foundation, 2010).

21. Ann Allen and David N. Plank, "School Board Election Structure and Democratic Representation," *Educational Policy* 19, no. 3 (2005): 510–27; Sarah F. Anzia, "Election Timing and the Electoral Influence of Interest Groups," *The Journal of Politics* 73, no. 2 (2011): 412–27.

22. Vladimir Kogan, Stéphane Lavertu, and Zachary Peskowitz, "The Democratic Deficit in U.S. Education Governance" (EdWorkingPaper 20-196, Annenberg Institute at Brown University, Providence, RI, 2020).

23. Brendan Bartanen et al., "Mapping Inequalities in Local Political Representation: Evidence from Ohio School Boards," *AERA Open* 4, no. 4 (2018): 1–19.

24. Christopher R. Berry and William G. Howell, "Accountability and Local Elections: Rethinking Retrospective Voting," *Journal of Politics* 69, no. 3 (2007): 844–58; see also Vladimir Kogan, Stéphane Lavertu, and Zachary Peskowitz, "Do School Report Cards Produce Accountability Through the Ballot Box?" *Journal of Policy Analysis and Management* 35, no. 3 (2016): 639–61.

25. Julia A. Payson, "When Are Local Incumbents Held Accountable for Government Performance? Evidence from US School Districts," *Legislative Studies Quarterly* 42, no. 3 (2017): 421–48.

26. Kogan, Lavertu, and Peskowitz, "The Democratic Deficit."

27. Kenneth J. Meier et al., "Structural Choices and Representational Biases: The Post-Election Color of Representation," *American Journal of Political Science* 49, no. 4 (2005): 758–68; Kenneth J. Meier and Amanda Rutherford, "Partisanship, Structure, and Representation: The Puzzle of African American Education Politics," *American Political Science Review* 108, no. 2 (2014): 265–80.

28. Hugh Macartney and John D. Singleton, "School Boards and Student Segregation," *Journal of Public Economics* 164 (2018): 165–82.

29. Bruce D. Baker, Danielle Farrie, and David Sciarra, *Is School Funding Fair? A National Report Card* (Newark, NJ: Education Law Center, 2018).

30. C. Kirabo Jackson, Rucker C. Johnson, and Claudia Persico, "The Effects of School Spending on Educational and Economic Outcomes: Evidence from School Finance Reforms," *The Quarterly Journal of Economics* 131, no. 1 (2016): 157–218; Julien Lafortune, Jesse Rothstein, and Diane W. Schanzenbach, "School Finance Reform and the Distribution of Student Achievement," *American Economic Journal: Applied Economics* 10, no. 2 (2018): 1–26.

31. Bruce D. Baker, "School Finance and the Distribution of Equal Educational Opportunity in the Postrecession US," *Journal of Social Issues* 72, no. 4 (2016): 629–55.

32. Interestingly, the source of inequities (whether within- or between-district) seems to vary by state. See Dan Goldhaber, Vanessa Quince, and Roddy Theobald, *How Did It Get This Way? Disentangling the Sources of Teacher Quality Gaps Across Two States* (Washington, DC: National Center for the Analysis of Longitudinal Data in Education Research, 2018).

33. Dan Goldhaber, Lesley Lavery, and Roddy Theobald, "Uneven Playing Field? Assessing the Teacher Quality Gap Between Advantaged and Disadvantaged Students," *Educational Researcher* 44, no. 5 (2015): 293–307.

34. Ibid., 293.

35. Dan Goldhaber, Vanessa Quince, and Roddy Theobald, "Teacher Quality Gaps in US Public Schools: Trends, Sources, and Implications," *Phi Delta Kappan* 100, no. 8 (2019): 14–19.

36. Sylvia Allegretto and Lawrence Mishel, *The Teacher Pay Penalty Has Hit a New High: Trends in the Teacher Wage and Compensation Gaps Through 2017* (Washington, DC: Economic Policy Institute, 2018).

37. James Cowan and Dan Goldhaber, "Do Bonuses Affect Teacher Staffing and Student Achievement in High Poverty Schools? Evidence from an Incentive for National Board Certified Teachers in Washington State," *Economics of Education Review* 65 (2018): 138–52; Thomas S. Dee and James Wyckoff, "Incentives, Selection, and Teacher Performance: Evidence from IMPACT," *Journal of Policy Analysis and Management* 34, no. 2 (2015): 267–97; Li Feng and Tim R. Sass, "The Impact of Incentives to Recruit and Retain Teachers in "Hard-to-Staff" Subjects," *Journal of Policy Analysis and Management* 37, no. 1 (2018): 112–35; Steven Glazerman et al., *Transfer Incentives for High-Performing Teachers: Final Results from a Multisite Randomized Experiment. NCEE 2014–4004* (Washington, DC: National Center for Education Evaluation and Regional Assistance, 2013).

38. Helen F. Ladd, "Teachers' Perceptions of Their Working Conditions: How Predictive of Planned and Actual Teacher Movement?," *Educational Evaluation and Policy Analysis* 33, no. 2 (2011): 235–61.

39. Ben White, "On Tax Day, Trump Tax Cuts Remain Deeply Unpopular," *Politico*, April

15, 2019, https://www.politico.com/story/2019/04/15/donald-trump-tax-cuts-unpopular-1273469.

40. Rucker C. Johnson and Sean Tanner, *Money and Freedom: The Impact of California's School Finance Reform on Academic Achievement and the Composition of District Spending* (Stanford, CA: Policy Analysis for California Education, 2018).

41. Brenda Iasevoli, "How Cities Are Convincing Voters to Pay Higher Taxes for Public Preschool," *The Hechinger Report*, May 19, 2019, https://hechingerreport.org/how-cities-are-convincing-voters-to-pay-higher-taxes-for-public-preschool/.

42. There are also union-related challenges to tinkering with teacher pay. However, it is generally accepted that there is a great deal more flexibility in teacher union contracts than is typically used. For a discussion of this issue and many relevant citations, see Joshua Cowen and Katharine O. Strunk, *How Do Teachers' Unions Influence Education Policy? What We Know and What We Need to Learn* (working paper 42, The Education Policy Center at Michigan State University, East Lansing, MI, 2014).

43. Allen and Plank, "School Board Election Structure"; Arthur J. Townlet, Dwight P. Sweeney, and June H. Schmeider, "School Board Elections: A Study of Citizen Voting Patterns," *Urban Education* 29, no. 1 (1994): 50–62.

DATA APPENDIX

1. Morgan S. Polikoff, "How Well Aligned Are Textbooks to the Common Core Standards in Mathematics?" *American Educational Research Journal* 52, no. 6 (2015): 1185–211.

2. Cory Koedel et al., "Mathematics Curriculum Effects on Student Achievement in California," *AERA Open* 3, no. 1 (2017): 1–22; Morgan S. Polikoff et al., *Curriculum Counts: Math and Science Textbook Adoptions and Effects* (Los Angeles, CA: USC Rossier School of Education Center on Education Policy, Equity and Governance, 2020).

3. Morgan S. Polikoff et al., "The Formalized Processes Districts Use to Evaluate Mathematics Textbooks," *Journal of Curriculum Studies* 52, no. 4 (2019): 451–77.

4. Koedel et al., "Mathematics Curriculum Effects."

5. David Blazar et al., "Curriculum Reform in the Common Core Era: Evaluating Textbooks Using Student Achievement Data," *Journal of Policy Analysis and Management* 39, no. 4 (2020): 966–1019; Shauna Campbell, *Disruptions to the Traditional Textbook Narrative: Lessons from District Leaders and Teachers in California* (Los Angeles, CA: University of Southern California, 2019).

6. Katie Pak et al., "The Adaptive Challenges of Curriculum Implementation: Insights for Educational Leaders Driving Standards-Based Reforms," *AERA Open* 6, no. 2 (2020): 1–15.

7. Morgan Polikoff et al., *Exploring Coherence in ELA Instructional Systems in the Common Core Era* (Santa Monica, CA: RAND, 2020).

ACKNOWLEDGMENTS

Six days after I moved to Nashville to start my PhD, in June of 2006, I went on a date with a handsome Vanderbilt admissions officer named Joel. We had sushi. He'd "slid into my DMs" (as the kids these days say) on Facebook, claiming to have read the book I'd indicated I was reading on my profile. It turns out he was making it all up because he thought I was cute. He told me about his little fib years later, but I didn't care because he was brilliant and charming and a true Southern Gentleman. This book is for Joel, the love of my life.

This book is also for my mom, Alyne. In 1992, when I was seven, my father passed away from brain cancer. My mom kept it together, held down her bank job (through merger after merger—she's still there today), and put dinner on the table every night. Over the years, she evolved to be my closest confidante. We still talk almost every day, and she's always the first person I turn to when I need wisdom. I couldn't have done this—or anything—without her support, guidance, and love.

* * *

Two years ago, I was sitting in my therapist's office and he said something like, "Morgan, you're bored; you need a challenge." Somehow, I convinced myself that writing a book was the challenge I needed. If you know me, you know I'm much more comfortable in the 280-character to 1,000-word range, so putting together 55,000 words or so seemed like a truly daunting task. But it's done, and I like it, and I hope you do too. Or at least, I hope you don't find it boring—that would be the worst. So, thanks to my therapist and on to the next challenge.

None of my academic success could have been accomplished without the training and ongoing support of my advisors Andy Porter and Laura Desimone. Andy is truly like a second father to me, and I am so fortunate that he brought us together. They have taught me all I know about how to conduct and report good research. And they have also been caring and supportive friends from Vanderbilt to Penn and beyond.

Along the way at the University of Southern California (USC) I've had support from some truly brilliant PhD students. They helped me carry out and write up much of the research you will read about here. Academia has a reputation as being a bunch of pointy-headed brainiacs sitting in empty rooms and theorizing all day, but for me it has always been a collaborative exercise. So, thank you to my PhD students: Stephani Wrabel, Matt Duque, Nan Zhou, Tenice Hardaway, Tien Le, Shauna Campbell, Hovanes Gasparian, Russell McFall, Shira Haderlein, Martin Gamboa, Sarah Rabovsky, and Dan Silver.

My academic home for a decade has been the USC Rossier School of Education. It's been a great place to be a scholar. Thank you to my deans—Karen Symms Gallagher and now Pedro Noguera—and the many collaborative colleagues I've worked with over the years.

This book could not have happened without the support of two specific people. First, I have to thank my friend Ethan Hutt. He advised me all the way through this process. He convinced me that I could do it when I was sure I couldn't. He told me it was good when I thought it was terrible. He's the most brilliant person I have had the pleasure of working with, but he's also a true, supportive friend. And second, I have to thank my editor, Caroline Chauncey. She approached me in May of 2017 wondering whether I might be interested in writing a book about standards. I told her not yet, but maybe soon. A few years later, here we are. She's been a steady, guiding hand, as well as a careful, critical eye throughout this process.

Last, much of the research in this book has arisen out of funded research, so I must thank my funders: the Institute of Education Sciences, the

National Science Foundation, the William T. Grant Foundation, the Bill and Melinda Gates Foundation, and an anonymous foundation. Research takes resources, and the generous support of these and other funders over the years has enabled me to do work that has, I hope, made a difference in education policy and practice.

ABOUT THE AUTHOR

Morgan Polikoff, PhD, is an associate professor of education at the University of Southern California (USC) Rossier School of Education. He received his doctorate in education policy from the University of Pennsylvania in 2010 and his bachelor's in mathematics with a minor in secondary education in 2006. He has published more than forty peer-reviewed journal articles, with his research primarily focusing on the design, implementation, and effects of standards, curriculum, assessment, and accountability policies in American education. To investigate these issues, he has also been principal investigator or co–principal investigator on grants totaling more than $15 million. In 2017, for his work on these topics, he received the Early Career Award from the American Educational Research Association (AERA). A committed public scholar, he also received the AERA Outstanding Public Communication of Education Research Award in 2020. He has been an associate editor of the *American Educational Research Journal* and a co-editor of *Educational Evaluation and Policy Analysis*. He has also been awarded by both USC Rossier and USC for his mentoring of PhD students. A three-time trivia game show champion, Morgan lives in Los Angeles with his husband, Joel Hart, and their cattle dog mutt, Indy.

INDEX